Delphiniums

Delphiniums

Colin Edwards

J.M.Dent & Sons Ltd
London Melbourne Toronto

First published 1981
© Colin Edwards 1981

Printed and bound in Great Britain by
Richard Clay (The Chaucer Press) Ltd
for J. M. Dent & Sons Ltd
Aldine House   Welbeck Street   London

This book is set in Quadritek Times by
Altonprint, Alton, Hampshire

British Library Cataloguing in Publication Data

Edwards, Colin
Delphiniums.
1. Delphinium
635.9′33′111   SB413.D4

ISBN 0-460-04423-0

Contents

List of Colour Plates

List of Black and White Plates

Acknowledgments

Most of all to my wife, Joan, for not only typing all the drafts and helping me generally, but above all for her incredible forbearance in remaining a devoted partner in spite of my almost fanatical love of the delphinium for over thirty years.

To Nigel Moody my most grateful thanks for his time and patience in producing the photographs. Also to Patrick Booth for attending to the enlargements of the monochrome photographs.

To John Neave of Dagwood Farm, Elmswell, Bury St Edmunds for his permission to use material painstakingly produced by him over the years to provide the unique list of species.

A bibliography has not been included for I owe much to my library of the Delphinium Society's *Year Books* covering fifty-one years and containing as they do a unique coverage of the delphinium not to be found elsewhere. To its contributors both past and present I am exceedingly grateful.

1 Origin and History of the Delphinium

The modern delphinium is one of the most splendid of all garden plants. With its magnificent spikes in a whole range of colours—white and cream, purple and mauve, gentian, lavender, amethyst, a range of dusky pinks and, of course, every conceivable shade of true blue—it has few rivals among the wealth of beautiful flowers which bloom in the mixed border at the height of an English summer. The delphinium started to make its impact just before the turn of the century when it was christened 'The Queen of the Border' by its gardening and horticultural enthusiasts, and it has continued to grow in popularity ever since.

The commonly grown perennial delphinium is familiar to most gardeners, and this book will chiefly be concerned with the pleasures and problems associated with its cultivation. In this chapter we shall look at its development as well as touching briefly on the less well-known Belladonna delphiniums and the biennial delphinium, often incorrectly referred to as an annual, which are quite separate races.

Today's delphinium is a very different creature from the species from which it evolved, however. Like so many other garden flowers it has improved steadily over the years. Occasionally improvements have occurred by natural means but more often than not it has been man, impatient with evolution, who has brought them about. The latter part of this chapter will survey the transformations that have been brought about by hybridization, chiefly in England, France, the USA and latterly in the Netherlands.

Obscure Ancestry

Compared to many plant families, the family of delphiniums is quite small, although it is substantially larger than is generally supposed. The botanist, Wilde, estimates the number of species to be 300 whereas Bailey considers the total to be in excess of 500. Chapter 13 lists all the species for which definite information is available, and also contains a second list of other recorded species where full details are either absent or the information may be questioned. It is certainly reasonable to assume that, as the years pass, more species will be discovered, for the inquisitive botanist is constantly adding to the list.

It is impossible to say exactly when the first delphinium was discovered, named and recorded but it may have been *D. staphisagria*, some 2000 years ago. There can be little doubt that it was at this time that the plant was given the name by which it has become known: the immature floret in bud was thought, somewhat fancifully, to resemble a dolphin and from this picturesque Greek idea the Latin equivalent—delphinium —evolved.

Larkspur

One form of the so-called annual delphinium is *D. ajacis*, a rare native of the British Isles, but fairly common in parts of Europe. In attempting to name this species man again turned to the animal world for inspiration. It says a lot for the intimate botanical knowledge of our forbears in medieval England that their studies of both plant—and bird-life lead them to the inspired name of 'Larkspur', for they noted a similarity between the lark's claw and that part of the spur formation of the calyx of an individual floret. From this origin, then, came the name used widely nowadays for referring to annual delphiniums. Although generally known as annuals, and more often than not listed as such in seed catalogues, larkspurs are, more correctly, biennials.

The colour range of the larkspur is not as extensive as the hardy perennial delphinium but, over the past years, hybridists have created a true pink strain and also a colour almost bordering on magenta. Many different forms have been evolved and, unlike the delphinium, seed can now be obtained that will produce plants true to colour and form.

Belladonna Delphiniums

Belladonna delphiniums are a quite distinct race. It would seem that they arose as a natural mutation and could well have as their ancestors *D. elatum, D. grandiflorum* and possibly *D. cheilanthum. D. elatum* has thirty-two chromosomes whereas both the latter have sixteen, giving rise to a feasible theory of evolution since Belladonna delphiniums have forty-eight chromosomes. Like its probable ancestors this flower has single florets which are fairly small, but unlike the familiar perennial delphinium they are of a quite distinct branching habit.

Credit for the development and introduction of Belladonna delphiniums belongs almost exclusively to the Royal Moerheim Nurseries at Dedemsvaart in the Netherlands, for it was in 1909 that an Award of Merit was given to a plant which had mutated naturally at the nursery a few years earlier. The plant was named *D. moerheimi*. In its infancy it produced five stems, four of which were white and the remaining one was blue. Even more remarkable was the successful vegetative propagation of the separate parts of the crown, giving rise to the first blue Belladonna which was subsequently named 'Capri'.

Belladonnas have never been cultivated extensively. Their habit of growth tends to pose problems with staking and the very limited colour range in mostly single florets has not improved their popularity.

The Hardy Perennial Delphinium

The more familiar hardy perennials are the glamour plants of the delphinium family and their development is a fascinating example of early hybridization. What is clear beyond reasonable doubt is that *D. elatum* was one of the species involved in the original cross pollination which eventually gave rise to the familiar garden plant of today. It is pure conjecture to name the other species which may have been used in this union and, although there have been many theories, there is no real evidence. Moreover, it is not possible to say with authority how the union came about.

To complicate matters, however, the delphinium enthusiast is constantly lead to the conclusion that early botanists and hybridists may well have confused the identity of some species. *D. elatum* is similar, and indeed appears to be a near relative, to *D. exaltatum.* The former is to be found at high altitudes in a zone which runs roughly from the Pyrenees to Siberia, whereas the latter is found exclusively in the United States of America. Both species produce flowers in the form of a spike. This similarity has lead to speculation that *D. exaltatum* may have been used by hybridists in the early days, but this is hard to believe since all hybridization was being carried out in the old world and it does not seem logical that a species from the United States of America would have been used in preference to a plant readily available to the botanists of the day.

Moreover, to cloud the issue even more, *D. grandiflorum* may well also have played a part in a multiple cross. But as this species has become more generally known today by the alternative label of *D. chinense* we are lead to the unfortunate conclusion that if these early plantsmen were naming two identical species with different labels then we cannot truly rely upon their records. Indeed, to make matters even more difficult to digest, writers recording the work of early botanists often mention *D. formosum* as one of the likely ancestors of today's hybrids while suggesting that this species is made up of two types. I find this hard to swallow and believe that confusion has occurred between two different species of similar habit.

Writing in *Country Life*, in the edition dated 20 August 1910, the then gardening correspondent sensibly put the matter in perspective. He said that he had little doubt that there were other species involved apart from *D. elatum* and *D. grandiflorum*, and that multiple inter-crossing must have been freely adopted in creating the race of garden delphiniums then widely grown in English gardens.

My own researches correspond with this view, for I have been unable to find any conclusive evidence which would enable any one to describe the true origins with any degree of authority. Certainly much has been written on the subject by writers clearly intrigued by the problem, but like so many historical mysteries it is impossible to sort out fact from fiction, especially when some people are merely expressing an opinion based on assumption, or worse still on speculation, rather than fact. In the circumstances we must be content to regard as convenient the name *Delphinium elatum* which is now widely accepted as the label to be used when referring to the race of perennial garden hybrid delphiniums cultivated extensively throughout the world.

Early Hybridization

D. elatum clearly impressed a number of early hybridists in the mid nineteenth century—indeed it almost came to the point where the flower had something of a cult following—and it is interesting to look at some of the first attempts at improvement. Early hybrids were almost without exception single-flowered and of a violet colour, although there is a recorded example of a double form in 1815, which was said to be *D. grandiflorum.* Just how double the flower was is open to conjecture, as indeed must be its origin. But what does seem certain is the emergence of the first true garden hybrid, known as *D. barlowii,* at about the same time, for the plant was placed on the Botanical Register for 1837 by the Royal Horticultural Society. It would appear that a Mr Barlow of Manchester raised this chance seedling and a nurseryman reporting on its performance gave it the highest accolade. It is worth reproducing an extract from the contemporary report of the Royal Horticultural Society:

> We received the delphinium from a friend at Manchester several years ago under the name *D. barlowii* and we believe it to have been raised by a florist of that name in the neighbourhood of Manchester: undoubtedly, it is a hybrid production and we think the parents to be *D grandiflorum* and *D. elatum,* partaking in growth and flower of the character of both. It is a most ornamental and beautiful herbaceous plant and very easy of cultivation: it appears to flourish in any soil and situation. We have had plants in bloom throughout the whole summer and autumn, the principal stems sometimes attaining the height of 7 and 8 feet and many branches. We have sold plants of it to most of the nurseries in Great Britain. One description of the flower was that it was 'semi-double' of a most intense blue colour.

In spite of this promising start in England it was French nurserymen who, around 1850, were actively pursuing the development of the flower. One prominent nursery was Lemoine of Nancy and it was from here that much of the early work took place. They produced many hybrids, the majority of which were of double or semi-double form, although it is clear that the individual florets were quite tiny in comparison with today's hybrids. It was this firm, too, that considerably extended the colour range: at that time growers quoted Lemoine's hybrids as being lavender, sky-blue, mauve and combinations giving rise to such expressions as 'blue with mauve, rose and purple'. Even turquoise was said to have been seen, but here there must be reservations for this colour is so difficult to describe, and one feels that a certain amount of poetic licence must have been used by the grower. But, without doubt, Lemoine's greatest contribution to the improvement of the delphinium was his 'Statuaire Rudé'. This hybrid received an Award of Merit from the Royal Horticultural Society in 1908 and was described then as: 'Flower pale mauve, the outer petals tipped with pale blue, semi-double 2½ inches in diameter in a magnificent dense floral column over 2 feet in length.'

It was not until around 1880 that British nurserymen began to take more than a passing interest in the delphinium, when Kelway's listed for sale plants of their own raising. It is clear that, apart from selling some introductions of their own, many were from the French nurserymen; and it is also clear that they used French cultivars as their standby for breeding purposes, for they were unsuccessful in their attempts at hybridizing many of the species then available, although mention is made of *D. exaltum, D. formosum* and *D. grandiflorum.*

As with Lemoine's 'Statuaire Rudé', Kelway's name will be forever linked with one outstanding cultivar, 'King of the Delphiniums', which was for sale in quantity at the turn of the century and was still available commercially until the Second World War. A measure of its popularity was the extraordinary fact that no less than sixty-six horticultural nurserymen of the day listed 'King of the Delphiniums' in their catalogues. Kelway's immense influence on the popularity of the delphinium, particularly in the late nineteenth and early twentieth centuries, cannot be over-stated.

It is fair to say that Blackmore & Langdon's name is

17

synonomous with delphiniums among today's gardening public. Who could not fail to be impressed by their superb exhibits at the Chelsea Flower Show each year and indeed at other notable flower shows in England? This company had small beginnings, in 1901, when Mr C.F. Langdon started the famous nursery with his partner, Mr J.B. Blackmore, having served 'an apprenticeship' as gardener to an amateur delphinium enthusiast, the Reverend E. Lascelles. By general consent Blackmore & Langdon's nursery has made a greater contribution to the development of the perennial delphinium than any other individual or nurseryman, certainly in the twentieth century. Of course, they had one distinct advantage over earlier hybridists in that they had at their disposal such established cultivars as 'Statuaire Rudé' and 'King of the Delphiniums'. In fact the former was used extensively for breeding purposes and figures in the pedigree of most of their significant cultivars.

Amateur Hybridizers

Before the Second World War the amateur hybridist contributed little to the continuing development of the delphinium, but this was not to be the case during the post-war period. With the decline of the large specialist nursery—and, as I write, there are doubts about the future prospects of the commercial delphinium specialist—the role of the amateur enthusiast became ever more important.

The exception during the inter-war years was the contribution made by Watkin Samuel, a civil servant, with his Wrexham strain. He raised seventy cultivars which received awards after trial, but such was the overall size of his plants, often growing as high 10 ft (3 m) in ordinary garden conditions, that one nurseryman introduced them as 'hollyhock' delphiniums. They are not really suitable for the average smaller garden, because of their excessive height, although they were popular for a time in large gardens and public parks.

Frank Bishop was another extremely successful amateur raiser of improved cultivars, until he relinquished his status by joining Bakers' nurseries in 1946. Although he raised some significant cultivars before the Second World War it was really in the late 1940s and 1950s that he gained his greatest successes with such cultivars as 'Mrs Frank Bishop' (1946), 'Agnes Brooks' (1946), and 'Anne Page' (1950), all of which have proven constitutions. Later in the 1950s Bakers' introduced their 'Commonwealth Strain', and although these plants were quite lovely pastel colours, they proved to be of poor constitution; no doubt this was due to the introduction of 'Pacific' blood (which more of later). Perhaps the best-known cultivar to come from Frank Bishop's hybridization was 'Swan Lake' an off-white thinnish spike with a contrasting black eye. Since it was introduced in 1953 this has proved to be his most perennial plant, for it can still give good account of itself. Frank Bishop certainly contributed in great measure to the development of the delphinium and his quest for true blues, in the early days especially, had enormous impact.

It is ironical, however, that the cultivar which has proved to be one of the best delphiniums since the war was a chance seedling raised by Ronald Parrett from a packet of seed he obtained from Bakers', labelled 'The Bishop Strain'. His 'Daily Express' was a lovely pale sky-blue cultivar of exceptional vigour, and such were its outstanding characteristics that it dominated the London shows for many years, especially in the 1950s, and was in great demand. It is still available today and has few rivals as far as the colour is concerned, although it must be said that it has now lost some of its vigour; this is hardly surprising in view of the fact that it first appeared over thirty years ago.

There have been significant contributions by other amateurs

since 1945. Mr J. Gilbert, the gardener to Mr H.R.N. Rickett, produced a number of interesting seedlings with very prominent eyes. Often of a contrasting colour the eyes were referred to as 'petalled'. Unhappily, with Mr Gilbert's sudden death, this line of breeding soon came to an end and is virtually non-existent today.

The late H.R. Lucas, known to most people in the delphinium world as 'Reg', was a leading light of the Delphinium Society for many years until his death in 1975. He grew a number of fine seedlings and outstanding among these were 'Joyce Roffey' and 'Hilda Lucas'. The latter cultivar, raised in 1961, is still the finest of all the late flowering delphiniums, which says much for its longevity and constitution. It is an extremely valuable plant for it blooms long after the first early cultivars have shed their florets and has no rivals as a late exhibition plant.

The most important advances in the field of amateur hybridization, however, were those of Tom Cowan. His cultivars have had an enormous impact in the delphinium world, rivalling the best produced by professional nurserymen, for a large proportion of his flowers have highly desirable attributes which cannot be found in delphiniums from other sources.

'Loch Nevis', for example, one of his finest plants, is quite outstanding in its virtues. Of a slightly deeper sky-blue than 'Daily Express', it has a smallish contrasting white eye and, although the individual florets are not of the highest order, it makes up for his slight imperfection by other qualities. It has a most important characteristic of retaining its bottom florets in perfect condition until the top ones are fully open; in fact, the tendency is for the florets to wither on the plant and not to shatter, thus extending the time during which it presents a beautiful appearance. Moreover, it produces upwards of 3 ft (1 m) of actual flower spike with very little extra by way of cultivation, and I know of no other cultivar which can with-stand the effects of the severest of summer storms so well without damage. Apart from being superb as a garden plant, where it never fails to create admiration, it has also been one of the most successful exhibition cultivars of all time. 'Loch Nevis' has completely dominated the shows in London for many years—so much so, in fact, that an abortive attempt was made to place it in an exclusive class by itself.

Tom Cowan has raised many other fine delphiniums, including some much sought after for flower arrangement such as 'Spindrift', 'Gossamer' and 'Les Sylphides'. A measure of his contribution can be judged by the fact that he has so far received no less than eight awards for his plants from the Royal Horticultural Society.

There are also younger amateur hybridists coming to the fore, and already Roy Latty has made considerable headway, notably with a range of 'pinks'.

The United States of America

Important work on the development of the delphinium has taken place in the United States of America, as well.

Luther Burbank, regarded by many as the greatest of all American plant breeders, took up the challenge towards the end of the nineteenth century by importing seeds from nursery-men in Europe. He raised many fine plants, but none appear to have made a sufficient impression on growers to stand the test of time. It was in 1912 that N.I. Vanderbilt, a President of the now defunct American Delphinium Society, used plants raised by Luther Burbank as a basis to make crosses with species to be found in the United States of America, notably *D. scopulorum*. The progeny became known as the 'Vanderbilt hybrids' and were popular at about the time of the First World War.

But to all enthusiasts the name of Frank Reinelt, a Czech who emigrated to America in 1925, will be forever linked with the 'Pacific' strain of seeds. In his native Czechoslovakia he was a gardener to one of the Royal households and acquired a wide knowledge of plant breeding which was to stand him in good stead. As early as 1930 his 'Pacific' strain was offered for sale by a nurseryman, but it was in 1934, when he became a partner with a Mr Vetterle, that his fame spread to Europe.

Reinelt's unique contribution came about in two ways. Using mainly seeds raised in England with some from Mr Vanderbilt, he set out on a planned programme of line breeding, with the aim of producing a series of strains which would give rise to plants each being of similar habit and colour. That he succeeded so well is a tribute to his understanding of the delphinium and his skill as a hybridizer. He introduced further blood at a later date by using seed of separate strains from two fellow Americans—Dr Leonian and Charles Barber. As a result his firm was able to offer an incredible range of separately packed seeds covering an enormous galaxy of colours, except yellow and true pink. These Pacific strains became universally admired in the United States of America and Europe—especially in the United Kingdom.

Reinelt's attempt to obtain a strain of *elatum* type red delphiniums was unsuccessful, however. Although he was able to achieve a cross by artificial means between *D. cardinale*, a red species with sixteen chromosomes, and *D. elatum*, with thirty-two chromosomes, the dominant colour of the progeny was far from being the scarlet colour which was his aim. One extraordinary by-product of his work, resulting from the infusion of *D. cardinale* blood into many of his strains, was an enhancing of richness in the colour of the florets, notably in the purple range.

To many growers in the United Kingdom Reinelt's most significant work lead to the 'Astolat' range of seed within the

Pacific strain which was then the nearest colour to pink available. From his original strain of 'Astolat' there have been many fine dusky pink cultivars produced in the United Kingdom, notably 'Janet Lucas' raised by Reg Lucas shortly after the Second World War. This produced remarkable spikes of a deep strawberry pink colour, often with 3ft (1 m) of flowering spike. Unhappily the plant failed to be long-lived and, although it was increased easily by vegetative means, its vigour steadily declined to a point where it became worthless and was then abandoned.

While it is clear that 'Pacific' blood has been introduced at some time or another into the ancestry of some important cultivars available today it must be stated that, as a separate unadulterated strain, plants raised from his seed do not possess any great degree of perenniality when grown in the United Kingdom and on the whole tend to have weakish stems, easily broken in our summer storms. This in no way reflects adversely on Frank Reinelt's work, for he never attempted or even desired to introduce longevity. His one aim was to produce seed strains in separate colours suitable for the balmy climate in parts in parts of the United States of America, where the seed could be sown in early spring with the certain knowledge that by the summer of that year these sowings would produce exceptionally fine spikes. In this goal he succeeded brilliantly, and even in the United Kingdom his strains could be relied upon to produce a representative display by late summer/early autumn, if sown in heat in early spring. Seedsmen in the United Kingdom quickly realized this potential and the label 'Pacific Giants' was soon displayed prominently in their catalogues and on seed packets.

Frank Reinelt retired from active work in the nursery in California in 1970 and there is now no true strain of 'Pacific' seed available, for the complicated and painstaking annual breeding programme necessary to maintain and fix the progeny was abandoned. Thus the seed now available under the label of 'Pacific Giants', in whatever colour offered, is merely seed saved from plants several generations removed from the original 'Reinelt' strain. Exhaustive controlled experiments with such seed prove beyond doubt that the plants produced are woefully inferior to the original strain, with little or no perenniality. They should be treated, in my experience, as an annual at best.

Finally, the lesser known 'Connecticut Yankees' are also available, a strain of seed originally raised in the United States of America by Edward Steichen using, among other species, crosses between *D. elatum* and *D. belladonna* hybrids. The result is an unusual form of dwarf delphinium, usually single, but growing as a clump of short spikes needing little or no staking. There is a tendency for this strain to produce plants capable of throwing several flushes of bloom in one year but, rather like the so-called 'Pacific' strain, they rarely survive in our climate for more than one year, and those which do seldom retain their seedling vigour.

The Netherlands: University Hybrids

The most significant attempt to produce colours other than blues, mauves, purples and whites in *elatum* form has occupied Dr R.A.H. Legro of the Wageningen University in the Netherlands, for the past twenty-five years. His researches are a fascinating example of the work of a dedicated plant breeder. It was in 1953 that Bob Legro and his staff first contemplated the enormous challenge they faced and their early endeavours to cross the wild red-flowering species were made with selected cultivated forms of *D. elatum*. He readily admits that the first five years were little more than a period of trial accompanied by the usual proportion of error, but he persevered.

The wild plants used in his effort to introduce warmer colours were the Californian orange-red species *D. nudicaule*, which has small branching habits, and the very much taller, intensely scarlet *D. cardinale,* which is also a native of California. These two species were crossed one with the other to produce hybrids inheriting the character of both parents; the number of chromosomes in each cross was sixteen. In order to cross the progeny of these hybrids with *D. elatum*, which has thirty-two chromosomes, Bob Legro used colchicine.* The experiment was successful, for the treatment achieved the doubling required and so the cross was made leading to the first authentically recorded hybrid of an *elatum*-like delphinium bearing pinkish-red semi-double florets with thirty-two chromosomes.

But it soon became clear that there was still a long way to go in the quest for a red, pink or orange garden delphinium. In 1961, realizing the formidable task ahead, Bob Legro sought the advice of the Delphinium Society and through the good offices of George Cairncross, an official of the Society, he met Brian Langdon of Blackmore & Langdon Ltd. The advice given was 'to go for constitution' and this has been one of the guiding principles—not that it has been easy to find, especially in those early days. The period from 1963 until 1968 was characterized by attempts to extend the genetical variability, particularly in the pink and red shades. There was general progress but it was clear that a more accurate method of assessment was required, in addition to the existing practices of counting the number of florets per spike as well as noting shades of colour by reference to the Royal Horticultural Society's colour chart. From 1965

* **WARNING**—The drug colchicine is an extremely poisonous substance requiring great care and expert handling and is obtained from the plant *Colchicum*, commonly known as the 'Autumn Crocus'. It is used in minute doses to bring about tetraploid plants whose cell nuclei possess double the normal number of chromosomes.

data about plant height, spike length and character of flower were collected and recorded, and since then no fewer than 10,723 plants, covering thirteen generations, have been grown and registered by Legro and his team.

In the early seventies the length of flower spike began to show considerable improvement: the average size exceeded 19 in. (50 cm) and by 1974 this had increased to 26 in. (64 cm). Progress continues in this direction and the University Hybrids have now reached a length where they compare favourably with the *elatum* cultivars. The size of individual florets has also improved considerably, and some of the latest seedlings have florets of similar size to modern cultivars. In general there has been a steady improvement over the years, with the current results being dramatically better than the early days. Constitution has been doubtful in the past—meaning the characteristics of hardiness and perenniality—but even in this direction there seem to be grounds for cautious optimism. Orthodox vegetative propagation has not been very successful so far, but tissue culture could possibly prove to be the answer in the future. Certainly colour has been fixed, for very nearly every shade of red, magenta, pink and even orange are now the rule rather than the exception.

So, is the red garden delphinium 'just around the corner'? It could easily happen within the next year or two, but there looms on the horizon the gloomy hand of economics. As Dr Legro said in a lecture given in 1978 in London:

> The smile of the early fifties is fading and the blue sky is turning cloudy. Not because I do not have faith in the final success—for that, the results achieved are too obvious—but lack of sufficient support for our ideas and stiffer evaluation of research priorities in Holland may soon force us to give up this fascinating subject.

It would be tragic if lack of funds prevented further research, when an *elatum*-like hardy red delphinium is almost with us. Let us hope that some way can be found around this problem.

2 Delphiniums from Seed

We saw in Chapter 1 that the delphinium is a complex hybrid so it follows that, generally speaking, a packet of seeds will produce plants which will vary enormously, not only in colour, but in form and habit. Raising delphiniums from seeds is both easy and rewarding. It is the source from which the seeds are obtained that is the vital consideration, and it cannot be emphasized too strongly that you select your seeds carefully from the various strains available, bearing in mind the nature of the parent plants involved.

Most of the seeds you will obtain from commercial sources have been gathered from plants which have been self-fertilized. This is a perfectly acceptable method for producing seeds in the vast quantities required for trade purposes. If the seeds have been harvested from plants of recent origin which have been given an award by the Royal Horticultural Society after trial at Wisley, then you are reasonably certain of a strain which will produce satisfactory results.

It is a fact, however, that the majority of plants at present on trial, and those which have been given awards over the past few years, are from amateurs; and, with the exception of one or two named cultivars which have been taken up commercially, the majority of these amateur-raised plants are not available to the trade. Thus the strains offered commercially will not include seeds from these successful amateur-raised plants, and they will be poorer as a result.

It is also a well-established fact that self-pollinated seeds from some fine named cultivars such as 'Blue Nile', 'Guy Langdon', 'Strawberry Fair' and 'Loch Nevis' will produce only very moderate results at best and more often than not miserable plants of poor appearance and constitution. A reliable nurseryman will, it is hoped, be aware of these shortcomings and will omit these cultivars in their mixed packets of seeds.

Worse still are seeds which have been harvested from random seedlings, for disappointment is bound to result. In fairness it must be admitted, again because of the complicated pedigree of the delphinium, that there is always the chance, albeit small, of the odd plant turning up which is worthwhile.

Growers in the United Kingdom or in similar climates should also consider the question of perenniality. Any seeds bearing the label 'Pacific Giants' are unlikely to produce plants suitable for these climates, as we saw in Chapter 1, and such plants will generally be of poor constitution and extremely short lived. Even packets not labelled as such may well contain seeds which have some 'Pacific' blood somewhere in their pedigree. The reputable seedsman will only include seeds of this nature from proven cultivars and, in any event, the proportion is likely to be quite small.

It is thus important to select very carefully those seeds which have as their origin the so-called 'English' strain, that is to say, which come from nurseries where attention to perenniality has been given priority over other attributes. In this connection the Blackmore & Langdon pedigree is supreme.

Seed Suitable for Warmer Climates

The question of perenniality is of no great importance in countries which have higher average temperatures than the United Kingdom. The method found to be most satisfactory in these cases is to treat all delphiniums grown from seeds as annuals. In addition to the 'English' strain 'Pacific Giants' will also be suitable, but only if obtained from authentic sources.

It could be argued that, if treated as an annual, 'Pacific Giants' have the advantage that, on the whole, they tend to mature more quickly from seed. But it is only fair to mention that experiences both in the United Kingdom and the United States of America tend to support the view that, while the 'Pacific' strain did have a larger range of pastel colours, their constitution was generally more fragile and they were certainly more prone to fracture in summer storms.

The reader may be puzzled by my use of the past tense in the preceding paragraph when, in fact, 'Pacific Giant' seed is still offered for sale. But, as we mentioned in Chapter 1, it is no longer possible to obtain a true strain so seeds which are offered under this label cannot, by definition, be pure 'Pacific Giants'; they will produce plants which are vastly inferior to Frank Reinelt's original range.

Choosing a Strain True to Type or Colour

We have already seen that an enormous range of colours and characteristics can be expected from a general seed mixture.

By careful line breeding it is possible partly to fix a strain of seeds so that a fair proportion will produce similar characteristics to the parent or parents. This is certainly the case with short delphiniums. Many years ago Blackmore & Langdon were able to introduce a strain from which you could expect a fair number of delphiniums to be less tall than from a general mixture. Other seedsmen have also offered shorter strains, sometimes referred to as 'dwarfs', but these have not been available for a sufficient time to evaluate their potential. One strain currently listed, 'Blue Fountains', appears to produce shorter plants, but the proportion with single florets would seem to be excessive.

It is also possible, to a limited extent, to produce a strain of seeds from which you can expect the majority of blooms to come true to colour and, in recent years, it is to a small group of dedicated amateurs in the Delphinium Society that much credit can be given for the advances in this field of line breeding.

White delphiniums can certainly be obtained from some strains, although the quality of the plants raised is generally rather poor and experience has shown that many have important characteristics missing.

The 'pinks', on the other hand, are one group which can be relied upon to give an exceptionally high proportion of plants similar in colour to the parent or parents. They are not a true unadulterated pink—the term 'dusky pink' has been coined to suggest a pinkish tone with a faint underlying flush of violet—but this is a minor qualification, for they make superb garden plants in a wide range of pinkish shades.

Another recent success, again by an amateur, after many years of crossing and inter-crossing, has been the production of a strain which gives rise to a remarkably high percentage of true blues; the majority are blue selfs (that is to say, the florets do not have, to a significant degree, any trace of other colours).

Hand-Pollinated Seed

So far in this chapter we have been considering seeds obtained from plants which have set seeds naturally, without inter-ference from man. Such seed is known as 'selfed', a term introduced to indicate that the seed pods have been formed by a self-fertilizing process. But, without doubt, the chances of producing a real 'winner' are increased dramatically by obtaining seed from a *deliberate* cross between two different cultivars. Indeed, one can say with certainty that in recent years the majority of named cultivars receiving awards after trial at Wisley were from deliberate crosses.

It is not easy to obtain seed of these newer strains, for they are not listed by the larger seedsmen. As they represent such a tremendous advance, however, it is well worth making the effort to find a source of supply.

Sowing Seeds

The successful raising of delphiniums from seeds is simplicity itself, providing certain vital procedures are followed. Failure to observe any one of them is a recipe for disappointment so before going any further I have listed them in order to emphasize their importance:

1 Correct storage of seeds before sowing—in cool conditions to preserve viability.
2 Covering the seeds with only the merest trace of compost.
3 Keeping the container in which the seeds have been sown in a temperature of not more than 60°F (15°C).

Lack of success in germinating delphinium seeds can often be traced to incorrect storage, but if we follow the pattern created by nature we shall be well on the way to preserving the seeds' viability. The delphinium is largely alpine in origin so the natural order of events is for the seeds to set in the autumn and then drop to the ground; low winter temperatures follow almost immediately and more often than not there is soon a covering of snow. The seeds remain in this cold environment until spring, when they will germinate in the warm, moist conditions.

It can be seen, therefore, why delphinium seeds deteriorate very rapidly when kept in warm conditions. Hermetically sealed packets assist in keeping viability high, but even in these circumstances seeds suffer in heat. The finest place to store them is in a domestic refrigerator—not the freezer compartment, but the general storage area—where they will retain their germinating powers for several years.

Why, then, do so many gardeners still have difficulty germinating seeds, even when they have stored the packets in their refrigerators? The damage, I suggest, has probably been done before the seeds were even bought. They may have been purchased from a shop or garden centre where the packets were on show in a very warm atmosphere, for example, or, worse still, where the sun's rays fell upon them. Moreover, our postal authorities may have unwittingly added to the problem. However well stored by the seedsman, all is lost if the postman's sack containing your seed is placed against a hot radiator.

When freshly harvested in the late summer and early autumn delphinium seeds will germinate freely, and many enthusiasts sow their seed then for this reason. However, if properly stored, seeds will germinate just as well if sown the following spring. There are advantages in either method and it is really a question of personal preference.

Autumn Sowing

Select a suitable container—flower pot or seed tray—and decide which type of seed compost you are going to use. Personally I find that traditional soil-based composts of the John Innes type give better results than peat-based ones, although these days they are, unfortunately, very variable in quality. Many growers use ordinary garden soil to which some sharp sand and peat has been added, with perfectly satsifactory results. One tip I can unhesitatingly recommend is a sprinkling of finely ground bonemeal: for reasons unknown to me the subsequent root structure is vastly superior to seedlings grown in a compost to which the equivalent 'dose' of a phosphatic chemical fertizier has been added.

The seed is large enough to be distributed evenly over the surface of the compost at about 1 in. (2.5 cm) intervals. The

i 'Loch Torridon'

ii 'Fanfare'

iii 'Guy Langdon'
(Both pictured in the author's garden)

iv 'Loch Nevis'

v 'Olive Poppleton'
   *(Both pictured in the
   author's garden)*

vi Delphinium border at Clack's Farm

vii Mr C. R. Broan's garden at Eastcote, Middlesex

next stage is vital. No more than the merest trace of compost should be used to cover the seeds. A utensil similar to a domestic flour sieve, or one using standard gauge perforated zinc, is ideal for dispensing a fine covering. If the odd seed remains on the surface leave well alone and do not be tempted to add a sprinkling more. The deeper sowing of seeds is a cause of failure.

Now place the seed container in a polyethene bag, or put a sheet of glass on top if you favour more traditional methods, and keep it away from the direct rays of the sun. High temperatures must be avoided: seeds' ability to germinate will diminish in inverse proportion to a rise in temperature. Aim at maintaining conditions of 50-60°F (10-15°C), although a degree or two either way is no cause for alarm. The temperature in the average greenhouse will obviously be far too high; on sunny days a reading of 70°F (21°C) and upwards would spell certain death to the seed. A cold frame against a north wall is ideal. Equally suitable is the shade cast by a shrub: place the receptacle underneath it.

Once the seed has germinated, however, the seedlings should be given a less shady environment. Again, aim at keeping the vulnerable young growths as cool as possible.

As soon as the seedlings have developed their first true leaves they are best transplanted, ideally into separate pots of about 3 in. (7.5 cm) diameter, though a box deeper than the average seed tray may be used instead. Again, a traditional soil-based potting compost is best. If you are content with modern peat-based alternatives you may wish to use these in preference, but I am bound to say that I find delphiniums grown in John Innes compost seem to 'get away' better when planted out. It may have something to do with the different root structures which develop in different media.

With these autumn-sown plants there is little to do other than ensuring that the compost remains moist at all times: it is difficult to kill a delphinium by over-watering, unlike many other plants grown in pots. The plants remain out of doors and as the days become cooler and the nights longer so the top growth will die down to the point where, in mid-winter, there is no visible growth left. Do not fear! Tiny eyes will have formed below soil level. With the lengthening days of early spring, and rising temperatures, these tiny dormant eyes will break and new growths will soon be apparent. These tough winter-hardy young plants will be ready to set out in their flowering positions as soon as your own particular soil is in a suitable condition for them.

There can be no hard and fast rules on the planting-out date, for soil and aspect vary enormously throughout the United Kingdom and, indeed, all over the temperate world. Perhaps somewhere from March to April may be considered as average. These autumn sowings will steal a march over the later spring sowings by producing quite a large spike of the average length of a mature plant in late June or July—depending, of course, on the skill of the gardener.

Spring Sowing

The advice given on autumn sowing applies in the main to seeds sown in the spring. The one essential difference is the use of some form of artificial heat if a sowing is contemplated in February or March.

A gently heated greenhouse is ideal and a small propagator is a useful accessory. Again, aim at temperatures of 50-60°F (10-15°C) for germination. Higher temperatures can be tolerated once the seedlings are growing away, and they can usefully be left in the coolest part of the greenhouse until they are developed enough to be hardened off in the usual manner and planted out in their flowering positions.

These sowings, made in gentle heat, should ideally be

transplanted into 3 in. (7.5 cm) pots. By early May the pots will be nicely filled with roots. Once planted out they will grow away at a prodigious rate, to bloom with a representative spike in late summer or early autumn

Later sowings can, of course, be undertaken with complete confidence even using a cold frame or a box with glass or plastic sheeting on top to create humidity. These plants will, however, be hard put to bloom in the year of sowing, although the odd precocious youngster may reward you with some colour.

3 Cultivation

Few plants respond to generous treatment as well as delphiniums. Even grown merely for garden decoration they will astonish you with their potential if you give them that 'little extra' and prepare the site as you would for a good crop of vegetables. Of course, they will survive if planted in ground which has been neglected, but just to shove them in some odd corner is a tragedy, for they will never produce anything but a shadow of their full glory. After all, if they are taking up space, why not grow them well?

The difference between a properly grown plant and one which has been left to its own devices is astounding. In the former case upwards of six spikes per plant, each bearing 3 ft (1 m) or more of bloom, are easily obtainable, whereas in the latter, a miserable plant of straggly appearance, with a mass of poor undernourished blooms 18 in. (45 cm) or so in length and requiring complicated staking, is all that will be produced.

Soil Preparation

Delphiniums thrive in a wide range of soils. A few years ago an interesting survey was carried out by the Delphinium Society to ascertain the nature of the soil where the most successful exhibitors had grown their prize-winning blooms. The results were surprising for they revealed an extraordinary range—heavy clay, loams of all kinds, sand, chalk, peat, hoggin, gravel—and one grower even described his land as London dirt. As one would expect, the pH values also varied widely.

Obviously in a book of this nature, it is not possible to cover every aspect of delphinium cultivation in all the different types of soil to be found in the United Kingdom or, indeed, the temperate world. The reader will need to make adjustments according to his own experience and circumstances, and in the light of his own soil structure. But some general guidelines can certainly be given.

It makes sense to look first at the conditions in which the ancestors of the garden delphinium thrive, because they survive quite happily in their natural environment without man's assistance. *D. elatum* was mentioned in the first chapter as almost certainly figuring in the modern delphinium's parentage: it is an alpine and requires sharp drainage with, at the same time, an abundance of moisture, which is provided by melting snow in its native mountain habitat. The soils in these areas are distinctly shallow, overlying rock, and *D. elatum* has accordingly evolved a shallow root structure consisting of a mass of fibrous roots which reach into the top 12 in. (30 cm) of soil to obtain maximum benefit from the profusion of moisture in the early months of the year. Examine the root structure of the modern delphinium and you will see immediately that it is similar to its ancestor: the most important part is uppermost, with a multitude of feeding hair-like roots.

Digging is a controversial subject, but the traditional advice to gardeners to dig their soil two spits deep obviously does not apply to the delphinium, because of the nature of its root structure. Although digging may help with drainage on very badly waterlogged soils, it only aggravates the problem on sharply drained soils. Not only does rain pass quickly through the top few inches, but it carried with it natural plant foods, especially nitrogen, and also the soluble fertilizers which we may add from time to time, so these benefits speedily bypass the delphinium's root system. It is far better to try to improve your soil's water-retaining capacity by surface cultivation only and to increase the depth of your soil by adding to the top. This is particularly important on thin soils overlying chalk. If you still feel it is vital to dig your soil, if only to add organic material to the top spit, then allow several weeks for the soil to settle before planting. Even then, consolidate the ground by treading.

Weed control is vital. Unlike most herbaceous plants delphinium resent disturbance, so much so that once planted and established they should on no account be moved, for they will never recover from the shock. Their permanent site must, therefore, be cleared of tenacious perennial weeds, either by cultivation or by using a modern total weedkiller.

Soil fertility. Before actual planting takes place consider the fertility of your soil. If you have constantly replenished the ground with organic matter then all will probably be well, but as a counsel of perfection I would always advocate a soil test by a competent authority. Soil varies so much from location to location that to generalize is to mislead. What can be stressed without fear of contradiction is the need for long-standing treatment, since the newly planted delphinium can well occupy the same site for many years. Coarse-ground bonemeal, which contains phosphates, will assist in producing a good root structure, and course-ground hoof-and-horn-meal is also very valuable for its long-term effects in supplying nitrogen.

Planting

Only one factor is vital: the younger the plant the better! This statement cannot be over-emphasized, for it is the key to long-term health and vigour, and, after all, we want our delphiniums to flourish in their positions year after year.

Without doubt the finest results will always be achieved by planting either young rooted cuttings (see Chapter 4) or seedlings which have been grown in 3-4 in. (7-10 cm) pots. (Care must be taken to ensure that the roots have nicely filled the pot, but the plant has not become pot bound.) At all costs avoid plants which have been dug up from the open ground, for such material will never recover from the shock and at best can only be treated as stock from which to obtain cuttings the following spring.

One exception to this rule of early planting is the treatment of eye cuttings (see Chapter 4). These young growths will still have the inherent vigour of orthodox cuttings if small plants can be obtained from pots in the early autumn: if planted at once they will establish themselves before the onset of cold weather. There is, in fact, irrefutable evidence that a young plant will continue to develop a root system well into December, in most years, for the soil remains insulated against the cold for longer than is generally supposed.

Set out your young, vigorous plants in the usual manner, a fraction lower than the soil level of the original container. Above all, plant them *firmly* in soil which is itself well consolidated. Nothing beats the heel and toe method and this should be used without fear providing, of course, that the soil is in a friable condition and not saturated with recent rain. It is far better to leave the plants in their small containers for a few days, where they will come to no harm, than to plant them in a sticky, wet clay. More plants are lost, or fail to give a good account of themselves, through loose planting than from all other causes put together. For ordinary garden display a planting distance of about 2 ft (60 cm) apart each way is about right, but for exhibition purposes a greater distance is desirable (see Chapter 8).

Now, if you are a gardener who has neither the time nor the inclination to improve your soil by supplying it with an adequate amount of organic material which will eventually convert itself into life-giving humus, then all is not lost. You can still grow good delphiniums!

If your soil has been neglected, great benefit will accrue from using, at the recommended rate, a balanced fertilizer which can be hoed into the top few inches after planting. Thereafter, keep an eye on the weather. If rainfall is sparse then watering *must* be carried out to encourage the young plants to make strong growth. (The gardener who has attended to the well-being of his soil will derive benefit from his endeavours in these circumstances, for organic matter will hold a reservoir of moisture and recourse to watering will be a rare necessity.)

As the summer progresses the aim should always be to encourage these young plants to make a strong root system. Delphiniums often surprise the novice by their rapid growth, especially if the soil has been treated in the prescribed manner.

A few weeks after planting it will be evident that your delphiniums are going to produce a flower spike. It is at this stage, in the case of rooted cuttings, that you must harden your heart and remove the tip of the plant which contains the embryo spike, using your thumb and finger-nail. In some cases the actual flower spike may have developed, especially if you have been absent for any length of time; this too must be cut out. The action of removing the embryo spike is to stimulate the root system into developing and producing tiny secondary growth at the base, below soil level, and which will soon appear above ground level. This activity is an indication that a sound foundation has been laid for the years ahead. Allow these secondary growths to develop and flower, which they will usually do towards the end of the season.

In the case of seedlings, particularly those grown for trial purposes, however, there are good reasons for allowing these plant to flower immediately (see Chapter 10). We know that the quality of delphiniums grown from seed is infinitely variable and we may well wish to ascertain their potential as quickly as possible, and not wait until the following year to see how good or bad the spikes may be. There is thus something to be said for letting a seedling bloom as speedily as possible in order to remove at once those plants which obviously fail to reach a required standard. My only reservation would be to suggest that, as soon as a selected seedling has been earmarked for growing on for another year, then most of the spike should be removed at an early stage, allowing only the bottom few florets to mature and set seed. By this compromise the plant has been given sufficient time to form substantial dormant eyes, so that the following year's display will not suffer to any great degree.

Subsequent Years

A plant that is a year old will produce several shoots or spikes in the spring following the year of planting—the number is utterly dependent on how well it has been grown the previous year—but it should not generally be allowed to carry all of them. Most delphiniums benefit from some degree of thinning at the start of the season, particularly those being grown for exhibitions (see Chapter 8). To clarify this statement and to indicate how impossible it is to be precise about this aspect of delphinium growing, I hope I may be forgiven if I digress for a paragraph or two.

At the Royal Horticulatural Society's delphinium trial grounds young rooted cuttings are planted in extremely well-prepared ground in late spring and the subsequent cultural treatment is, as you would expect, of the highest order. The result of this expert cultivation and rich diet is incredible: the following spring the crowns produced will be enormous and it is commonplace for one plant to have twenty or more shoots. In several instances I have counted no less than fifty shoots appearing just ten months after planting. This is, of course, an extreme illustration and the amateur should not expect to achieve phenomenal results of this kind. Indeed, it would not be desirable for ordinary garden purposes, for the aim at Wisley is somewhat different to that of the gardener.

On the other hand, a rooted cutting grown in poor conditions and neglected in its year of planting may well only produce one or two spikes the following year. It would be wrong, therefore, to be dogmatic about the question of the number of shoots to thin as clearly so much depends on the vigour of the plant. On a plant which has made poor growth it would be sensible to allow only one shoot to develop, whereas on a vigorous plant the thinning can be less drastic. Some growths may well be taken as cuttings in order to increase stock and, thereafter, all thin, spindly growths should be removed leaving only the strongest to develop and flower. It will be necessary to examine the plants over a period of several weeks, for shoots do not appear all at once. There is also something to be said for cutting out unwanted shoots over an extended period, building up a balanced plant as you proceed. Generally speaking all thinning should be finished before the growths reach a height of about 12 in. (30 cm).

Now is the time to apply a balanced fertilizer if you have doubts about the fertility of your soil because growth is disappointing. Choose a fertilizer with a high nitrogen content and a bias towards a formula which does not contain nitrate of soda, for this chemical can harm the soil structure. If you are satisfied that your soil has been well looked after and yet growth is still poor, it is possible that the nitrogen content is low. This can occur after very wet periods, for nitrogen is easily leached from the soil. For many years dried blood was advocated by leading delphinium growers and it is still an extremely valuable organic fertilizer for making good a nitrogen deficiency. However, it is expensive and similarly beneficial results can be obtained with a 'straight' fertilizer: sulphate of ammonia is relatively cheap and readily available.

Staking

Towards the end of April or the beginning of May, depending on location and season, the plants should be growing strongly and will be at a stage when they can be staked.

One favoured method for established plants is to use three stout canes in the form of a splayed triangle round which a proprietary soft tying material is wound in the form of a spiral. This is really the only satisfactory way in which to deal with six or more shoots. If thinning has reduced the number to three or less, then one cane to each shoot has some advantages, for a shorter cane of about 3 ft (1 m) can be used and one fairly tight tie should be made about 12-18 in. (30-45 cm) from ground level with another, much looser one, as the plant lengthens, at a point 12 in. (30 cm) below the bottom florets (see Plates 10 and 11).

The aim with all staking is to tie the stems securely at the lower end, but more loosely higher up so that the plants can sway in strong winds. On no account should a tie be made too tight on the upper part of the stems as this can create a whiplash effect with the danger of fracture, especially in summer storms when a spike in full bloom is laden with water. On short cultivars, where the bottom florets are often a mere 18 in. (45 cm) above ground level, little or no staking will be required.

There is little left to do after staking except to see that the blooms do not suffer through lack of moisture. A really good soaking will be appreciated in periods of drought.

Disbudding

As the spike develops a number of side shoots, known as laterals, will appear below the bottom flower buds. Some growers remove a number or all of these secondary growths on the grounds that this improves the main spike. If this is the case it can only be, in my opinion, a minimal factor and it is a great pity to deprive yourself of the lovely laterals which can be so useful in the home for flower arrangements (see Chapter 9). So my advice is to leave well alone and enjoy this bonus!

Care of Plants After Flowering

Perhaps the greatest mistake in delphinium cultivation is to neglect them *after* flowering. Yet this is a vital time to provide a good foundation for the future well-being of your plants.

Only the spent flower spikes should be cut away, leaving the stems to die down naturally before these too are removed in the autumn. No great harm will arise if a few withered florets are left to set seed, but do not leave more as this will exhaust the plant needlessly.

It is possible to achieve a second flowering by cutting the stems off at soil level immediately after blooming. This is not, necessarily, a wise action, but much depends on each plant. Some delphiniums, and specifically certain cultivars such as 'Blue Nile', 'Fenella' and 'Silver Jubilee', have this propensity to bloom more than once, fresh growth often being visible at the base while the plant is still in full bloom. In these circumstances do not hesitate to remove all top growth and encourage the welcome addition of further spikes later in the year. On the other hand to force a plant into secondary growth has a decidedly weakening effect and the following year's display will suffer, for the eyes will be forced into growth instead of remaining below ground to plump up for the following year.

45

Delphiniums

It is just as important to see that your delphiniums receive plenty of water *after* flowering as it is before. A good soaking in drought conditions during late July and August will help considerably in the formation of those fat dormant eyes which will provide next year's blooms.

During late autumn and early winter the plants can be generally tidied up, and the canes and weeds removed. Bearing in mind the relatively shallow root system of the delphinium and the fact that important fibrous roots are just below the surface, it is a mistake to use a border fork around them for roots will inevitably be broken. There is no implement like a dutch-hoe, or the modern equivalent, and this should be the only tool used once a delphinium has been planted. Even better, simply mulch the soil with as much organic matter as can be obtained: any material is suitable at this time of the year. I suppose it is just possible to 'overdo a good thing' with stable manure, but his is hardly a likelihood with such a scarce commodity.

4 Vegetative Propagation

We saw in Chapter 2 that it was not possible to raise from seed a delphinium cultivar similar in every respect to the parent from which the seed was obtained. Fortunately there are several other methods of increasing your stock of named delphiniums, and in this chapter we shall look at them in detail.

Cuttings

Taking cuttings is the propagating technique used universally by amateur and professional delphinium growers alike and, providing care is exercised, it is usually a straightforward process. It must be admitted, however, that although there is nothing difficult about it, a delphinium cutting will not root so readily or easily as a dahlia or a chrysanthemum cutting.

The gardener who only wants to increase his stock by a modest amount should examine his plants some time towards the end of February for, depending on the season or locality, this is when the most forward plants will begin to grow. If there are shoots visible then a start can be made (see Plates 21 to 25).

Taking great care not to damage these rather brittle young growths, gently remove the soil around the crown of the plant until you reveal the base of the shoots. Examine any growths which are between 2½ in. (6 cm) and 4½ in. (11 cm) long. Ignore any particularly fat or thin shoots and select one or more, according to your requirements, which looks marginally thicker than an average pencil. With a very keen blade sever the shoot at the point where it joins the hard crown and examine the cut end. If it presents a solid whitish appearance then you have perfect material. If there is the slightest indication of hollowness or there are brown or black marks in the tissue then it should be discarded. A hollow end would indicate that the shoot was cut too far away from the base and the discolouring is a potential sign of disease. Many of these unsatisfactory cuttings would, in fact, root, but they seldom form a crown and quickly rot away.

It is essential to stop the cuttings drying out. If there will be any delay in placing them in their rooting mixture, then keep them in a small vessel containing about an inch of water.

Of course, the whole process of taking cuttings continues week by week—sometimes in mild weather an almost daily inspection is required to keep abreast, as growth can be very rapid and you can 'miss the boat'. Some delphiniums, especially late cultivars, may not be sufficiently advanced until mid April. Cuttings taken at this time of the year will still be satisfactory and, in fact, will tend to root more quickly with the higher temperatures prevailing.

For those gardeners who are reluctant to scrabble about in the soil during what can be a very cold period—and I must admit that it is not the warmest of tasks—I would recommend lifting the whole plant in early February and removing it to the more congenial atmosphere of a greenhouse. This method is common in the trade, and with the amateur who wishes to take a considerable number of cuttings from one cultivar. Moreover, if crowns are lifted and placed under glass, with a little soil or peat around their root system, early in the year then a start may be made sooner. Spraying a jet of water onto the crowns facilitates removal of the soil and gives easier access to the shoots, and there is also the added advantage that cuttings may be taken over a much longer period, as and when they reach the recommended length. Take the cuttings exactly as described above. (As mentioned in Chapter 3, delphiniums resent disturbance so there is no point in replanting crowns lifted for propagation; they should be discarded once cuttings have been taken.)

There are several methods of rooting cuttings and a variety of pet theories have arisen, but whichever appeals the cutting should be prepared for this process in the same way. The aim should be to produce a clean cutting with a few tufts of partially opened leaves, so the base should be neatly trimmed to clean off any snags, and any leaves which have completely unfurled should be removed.

An Easy Method of Rooting—Water Cuttings

This method is comparatively new and is ideal if you only want to root a few cuttings. Simply take a watertight vessel, such as a clean fishpaste pot, fill it with about 1 in. (3 cm) of coarse sand and add sufficient water so that there is about ½ in. (1.5 cm) above the level of the sand. Place the cutting so that the base just nestles in the sand—and that is all there is to it. It matters little where the pot is kept, except to guard it from extremes of temperature. The shady part of a warm greenhouse is ideal, but a window-sill is perfectly adequate and many thousands of delphinium cuttings have been rooted this way. The level of the water should be inspected from time to time and topped up whenever necessary.

After an interval of between fourteen and thirty days the cuttings will begin to form roots (see Plate 26). One cannot be precise about the length of time, for temperature is important and some cultivars root more quickly than others. To observe the rooting process, either look through the glass or take out the cutting and replace it if no roots are visible. Once it is apparent that roots are being readily formed (Plate 28) immediate potting is vital, for the roots are very brittle at this stage. Use the compost of your choice in about 3 in. (7.5 cm) pots.

As these young plants have been nurtured in a warm place they must be gradually hardened-off, ideally in a cold frame. Keep the lights in position and then subject them to the normal hardening-off process until such time as they may be planted out in their permanent site.

The Orthodox Method of Rooting—the Cold Frame

Rooting delphinium cuttings in an unheated cold frame has been standard practice among amateur growers for many years. Simply place an inch or so of really sharp sand or coarse grit onto the soil in the frame and dibble the cuttings into the sand to a depth of about 1 in. (3 cm). Water thoroughly and allow the foliage to dry before replacing the frame lights.

It is important to guard the cuttings in the frame against extremes of temperature. The frame should be sited where rays of direct sunlight do not penetrate the glass; a north wall is ideal. Failing this, some form of shading must be given, such as green polythene whenever there is full sunshine, for the temperature inside the structure can rise very quickly. Excessive heat will dehydrate the growths to the point where rot can occur and the cuttings will die. In periods of cold weather, and especially on frosty nights, it helps to cover the frame with some form of protection such as sacking or, better still, expanded polyestyrene. This has marvellous insulating properties, but it must of course be weighted down.

It should not be necessary to water the cuttings during the rooting period, which will take from three to five weeks. But if the sand is felt to be excessively dry then it is essential to make certain that the foliage has dried after watering *before* replacing the lights.

An indication that rooting is taking place is often mistaken for a disaster by the novice. It is curious to observe, a day or so before the first roots are formed, a limpness in the cutting which can give rise to apprehension that all is not well. To rush for the watering can is a mistake, for excessive moisture on the foliage can so easily cause rotting. Be patient for, a day or so after this limpness, the small leaves suddenly become turgid—a sure indication that rooting is taking place—and subsequent growth will be rapid.

With the cold frame method there is no need to pot the rooting cuttings immediately: they can be allowed to push their roots into the soil below the sand for a week or two during which time a gradual hardening-off should take place. They may, of course, be removed and potted up straight away, especially as the frame may well be required for other purposes at what is a busy time of year for the keen gardener. Whatever method is adopted these young plants may be set into their permanent positions after a period of about five weeks from rooting.

If your cold frame is on concrete rather than soil, place your cuttings in containers filled with a rooting compost in the frame. There are many mixtures advocated, but as long as the media has good drainage and is capable of admitting air, all will be well. Horticultural grade vermiculite or similar inert materials are ideal. The only point to bear in mind is the speedy removal of the cuttings to a compost containing plant food once they have rooted.

Eye Cuttings

The rather more difficult technique of propagating delphiniums from eye cuttings has been known for some time, but it has only become popular with some growers in recent years (see Plates 19 and 20).

Delphiniums

The word 'eye' is somewhat misleading because it is used to refer to the dark centre of a floret as well as being the term by which most authorities now refer to the dormant shoots which form in a cluster on that part of the base of the flowering stem where it joins the crown. These 'eyes' form during the period before blooming and, as the main flowering stem begins to wither and die, so they gain in size. They normally remain dormant throughout the rest of the year, to provide the flowering stems for the following season.

However, eyes can be rooted in the summer months—which is certainly one advantage over the normal cuttings—and they can be used to increase stock rapidly. They are particularly valuable if you have a seedling which you feel has great potential. Normally you would have to wait until the spring following the year in which the seedling had bloomed before increasing the plant by taking cuttings. Eyes, on the other hand, may be used for increasing stock some three weeks after flowering, thereby saving one year.

To facilitate the removal of the cuttings it is best to dig up the plant and clean off all traces of soil, using a jet of water from a garden hose. As with orthodox cuttings the eyes should be taken as close to the crown of the plant as possible.

A hormone rooting powder can be useful in the warmer conditions prevailing. The active ingredient does not, I believe, assist in temperatures below 60° F (15° C) so it is doubtful if this chemical proves of any value with spring-taken cuttings. If the brand selected also contains a fungicide, this is all to the good, as it will help destroy any mildew spores which may be present.

The compost chosen should be similar to that used for spring cuttings. Take care, when placing the eyes in the compost, to insert them to a depth where the tip of the eye just appears above the surface. It is vital to site the container in a shady place, well away from the sun's rays, and the atmosphere must be kept close at all times. The compost should remain fairly moist, but never excessively so, for this could easily lead to rotting in summer temperatures and is the main cause of failure.

Hygiene is important with spring cuttings but it is essential with these tiny vulnerable growths in warm summer conditions. Always use compost, containers and knife blades that have been properly sterilized. It is all too easy to incubate a pan full of disease and end up with complete failure. In normal conditions rooting is quick, often inside three weeks, and is indicated by the appearance of tiny tufts of leaves. Potting into a small size pot should be undertaken fairly promptly if an inert compost is being used.

Treatment of the eyes after rooting depends very much on when they were propagated. If they were taken in the early summer months, then they will be sufficiently large to set into the open ground by late summer or early autumn. Later struck eyes are best left in their pots to die down naturally until the following spring, when they too may be planted as new growth appears, usually in early March.

It would be misleading to suggest that this method of propagation is easy to master, but the rewards can be high. An incredible number of plants may be obtained at one time: as an indication, I once took no less than thirty eyes from the base of one stem and successfully rooted twenty-five. A tremendous advantage can thus be gained, especially with a selected seedling in its maiden year.

'Mini-Minors'

Other growths which may also be rooted in the summer months are the young shoots which appear above ground level and are similar to spring cuttings. They have been labelled 'mini-minors', since they are dormant eyes which have been stimulated into growth, usually by the early removal at ground level of all shoots which have flowered. Follow the technique described for eyes to root these small shoots.

Division

Hardy perennial plants which may be increased satisfactorily by division have a mass of fibrous roots, clearly indicating that the plant will separate easily into portions, often by merely pulling away outside new growth from the central and older part of the original plant. The root structure of an established delphinium is, however, quite different. In the first year of planting the maiden delphinium will usually produce just one single flowering stem. The following year new growths will develop around the base of this part of the plant, leading to several stems. This process is repeated each year, with new growths appearing from the base of the stems made in the previous year. After several years a large clump will have formed, but the original central part is, for all practical purposes, lifeless.

Each and every stem is linked together by hard tissue called the 'crown' and the only way to divide the plant is to rupture the crown. If this is accomplished in early spring, using a knife—and it will need to be very sharp, for the crown is often extremely tough—then there is just a small chance of success. It is essential that the severed portion contains a stem surrounded by young shoots or dormant eyes.

Division was, in fact, the normal practice of delphinium nurserymen before the Second World War. They tried to control the almost inevitable rotting of the wounded portions by leaving them in the air for a few days so that a callous could form. Flowers of sulphur was often used to assist this process. They were fairly successful, by and large, but losses through rot were inevitable, despite the care exercised.

Division cannot, therefore, be really recommended as a viable propagating technique for the amateur, especially when taking cuttings is such a satisfactory method of increasing stocks.

5 Pests and Diseases

Fortunately the delphinium is a remarkably trouble-free plant, with one important exception: more losses are caused by the depredations of molluscous animals than all other causes put together. It is pointless attempting to produce fine delphiniums if steps are not taken first to reduce the population of slugs and snails to a point where they are, for all practical purposes, eliminated from the soil where delphiniums are to be planted.

Slugs and Snails

Of the two creatures slugs are the greater menace and the more difficult to control, for they are both hermaphrodite and protandrous (that is to say, when first mature they have the facility to function as males and later in their life-cycle as females). This dual sexual role means that each and every slug is capable of producing eggs.

There are many species of slugs. Some rarely enter the boundaries of the cultivated garden and may be ignored, but the most common species is *Arion hortensis* and it is often referred to as the 'garden slug'. It enjoys cultivated soil and can live both above and below ground; the eggs, which are little bigger than a pin-head, are opaque and usually laid in the autumn, hatching with the advent of warmer weather in the spring. *Agriolimax reticulatus* is known as the 'field slug', but do not let this definition fool you for it is quite happy in our gardens. It is the most widely seen slug, because it lives entirely above ground.

Its egg laying is prodigious for it can produce literally hundreds of translucent eggs over a very short period during spring, with the progeny hatching during late summer. *Milax budupstensis* is the final 'monster' we should consider. More often abundant in clay soils, it is the largest of the three species, measuring on average 3 in. (8 cm) and living both above and below ground. Its egg laying capacity is modest, since it seldom lays more than twenty opaque eggs which hatch in late spring and early summer.

It can thus be seen that slugs are active during all the milder months of the year and eggs can be laid over a long period, so a constant war must be waged on these pests, as well as on their eggs, except perhaps during the depths of winter. It is possible, with a determined approach, to keep matters under control and there are several methods open, but I shall omit any reference to the more dangerous chemicals for ecological reasons as well as for the danger these deadly poisons pose to both children and animals. The control of snails may be achieved by similar methods.

Physical measures of control. Slugs and snails find the shelter of almost any object to their liking: most of us will have lifted, say, a plank of wood from the surface of a neglected patch of soil to find many pests adhering to it. It is logical, therefore, to keep the garden as tidy as possible and to remove all debris from contact with the soil, thus depriving them of their hiding places and giving their natural predators the chance of a kill. Molluscs detest gritty substances and are not found to any great extent in soils naturally containing an abundance of sharp sand. A good way of keeping these pests from a delphinium is to surround the crown with a dressing of sharp grit or coarse weathered ash; but this does nothing to reduce the population.

Old fashioned remedies such as providing traps, either commercially made or in the form of an upturned half orange skin, certainly collect slugs and snails, but many such devices are required and regular inspection is essential for this method to be worthwhile. In the same category come zinc rings which can be placed around each plant. Certainly no slug or snail will climb this metal, but the rings are really valueless for they do nothing to prevent the burrowing slug from attacking the crown.

Chemical control. For many years metaldehyde has been used to provide a reasonable measure of control, usually in the form of pellets obtainable from most horticultural sundriesmen. More economical are 'meta' fuel blocks which can be bought from chemists or camping shops. Crush the blocks and mix the powder with a carrier, such as bran, at the ratio of one part to fifty. Both pellets and powder are placed adjacent to the plants; they are irresistible to slugs and snails and appear, at first sight, to be lethal. Unfortunately pests can recover completely from an intake of this poison, especially after a rainy period, which has given rise to the widespread view that metaldehyde is very limited in its effectiveness.

Now a new pellet is available, under several proprietary names, which contains methiocarb. This bait is remarkably efficient and accounts for the death of countless slugs, but unfortunately the poison also destroys worms which are, of course, a boon to the gardener. I am reliably informed that the chemical is not dangerous to domestic pets or birds. But clearly, with so much controversy over the use of chemicals, care should be taken with this product if children are about as it is 'better to be safe than sorry'.

The remedies mentioned so far are only effective against the slugs themselves. If the source can be attacked and the eggs destroyed before they hatch, the problem is greatly reduced. To this end the chemical aluminium sulphate is a very useful substance for it has the same dehydrating effect on adult slugs and their eggs; its astringent action literally dissolves both.

59

(Years ago it was used in its pure form as a mouth wash for dissolving ulcers.) The commercial grade should be dissolved at the rate of 2 oz (55 g) per gallon of water which will cover approximately 4 sq.yd (3.36 sq.m).

While there is no well-documented evidence to support any view that the solution is harmful to the plants, there are many who feel that it should only be applied during winter when the plants are thoroughly dormant, as it is thought that it may have a caustic effect on young growth. It is also unwise to use this chemical on acid soils for its action is to reduce alkalinity.

Caterpillars

The damage caused by this pest can be very irritating, but it seldom, if ever, reaches epidemic proportions. The most obvious sign that a caterpillar has been present is a damaged flower spike or, on occasions, its complete absence. Examine your plants during late May or early June *before* the spike is visible: the clearest indication of this elusive creature's presence is a curling or twisting of the immature leaves at the tip of the plant. If these leaves are prised apart the caterpillar can be seen, safely hidden from predators, in a cylindrical leaf which it has formed as a home from where it can feed on the embryo spike deep down in the growing area. Removing the offender by hand-picking in this way is one of the chief means of control, if you are vigilant and early enough.

To approach the subject in a more scientific way we need to examine the life-cycle of the creature. The so-called delphinium moth has been identified as *Polychrysia moneta* by some gardening writers, others have referred to it as *Tortrix cnephasia* while yet others have mentioned *Cnephasia stephensiana* as being responsible. It is probably that more than one species is interested in the delphinium, but most enthusiasts who have studied this subject will agree that

60

Polychrysia moneta is the worst offender and certainly the most common.

The moth lays its eggs in late spring or early summer and they hatch out some seven to ten days later. The immature caterpillar is dark brown, turning to a light leaf-green colour when fully grown (no doubt an evolutionary change to match its environment). It seems reasonably certain that some caterpillars remain as caterpillars, to over-winter in the hollow stems attached to the crown of dormant delphiniums. With warmer weather they become active and climb the new growths in anticipation of their first feed since the previous year.

Control. Apart from the hand-picking method already mentioned, there are grounds for recommending spraying a systemic insecticide on your plants early in the year, when growths are about 2-3 ft (60-90 cm) high. The spray will have to be repeated at intervals, in accordance with the manufacturer's recommendations, until the spike elongates and there is no longer any danger from caterpillars.

However, insufficient research has been carried out into exactly which chemicals may be safely used on the dormant crown. This is probably because, as the damage these pests can cause is never extensive, such research has a low priority. It does mean, however, that it is not possible to recommend any methods of control which are fail-safe.

It occasionally happens that a caterpillar may find a winter resting place in the hollow end of a bamboo cane used for staking, rather than the stem of the plant. In this case it can be destroyed easily, merely by dipping the ends of the cane in a suitable insecticide.

Very infrequently some damage may be caused in spring to young cuttings in the warm environment of a frame or greenhouse, if a hibernating caterpillar is brought in unwittingly in a dormant crown being used for propagation.

Perhaps the most sensible attitude to adopt is to accept damage to the odd spike philosophically. Some specialist growers never experience any trouble, and even in the worst cases the percentage of plants involved is really insignificant.

Other Insects

Apart from an eel worm, known as *Pratylenchus pratensis*, there are no other known insects which damage the delphinium, and eel worm attacks are so rare that they have never even been encountered by some people who have devoted a lifetime to growing delphiniums.

Mildew

Fortunately the spores responsible for the spread of this unsightly disease do not present any great problem for they do not generally appear until after flowering and even then they do not flourish, for most cultivars are immune. The darker colours, especially the purples, are considerably more prone to attacks and in these cases early bouts of mildew can appear while the plant is actually in flower.

Control. With a modern systemic fungicide mildew-susceptible cultivars can be sprayed in early June with the certain knowledge that complete control may be achieved. Prompt spraying is important: prevention is certainly better than cure. However, to keep matters in perspective, it is possible to grow a very wide range of cultivars which, for all practical purposes, are immune or practically immune from this trouble.

Rot

The collapse of the structure of a plant's crown is often mistakenly called 'blackrot' by British growers. My own researches indicate that true blackrot is a fungus which attacks plants peculiar to the United States of America and is a fatal disease which can spread alarmingly. I can find no evidence that there have been any significant recorded cases in the United Kingdom.

The rot experienced in this country is not a disease, but a degeneration of the crown's tissue leading to the death of the plant. There does not appear to be any authoritative work available to explain the causes of this malady. Some recent studies have been carried out by the Royal Horticultural Society at Wisley but the results are inconclusive.

My somewhat superficial enquiries among leading growers guide me to the view that the nature of the soil and its cultivation may well have a direct bearing on the incidence of rot in Britain. One hard fact has certainly emerged: rot is rarely encountered on sharply drained soil, such as sand or gravel. But do not immediately jump to the conclusion that a more retentive soil is likely to increase the problem, for several growers of my acquaintance garden on heavy clay and yet seldom experience trouble, and I even know of some splendid, longlived delphiniums grown in heavy soil which is regularly flooded each year in the winter, sometimes for weeks on end. We must, I feel, look elsewhere to explain this irritating problem suffered by some growers.

The practice of taking cuttings from a plant *in situ* may well aggravate the trouble, especially if steps are not taken to seal the inevitable wound left on the crown. There is definite evidence that bleeding can occur from such wounds and it is conceivable that on well-drained soils, which are naturally drier, the wound callouses over more quickly than in wetter conditions. It is possible, therefore, that plants may literally bleed to death with the subsequent collapse of the crowns which have lost their moisture content and dehydrated. I can only speak from experience in support of this, admittedly inconclusive, theory. I rarely take cuttings from plants growing in the border, but invariably lift the crown for this task and dispose of it when it has served its purpose (see Chapter 4). Rot is a problem that I seldom encounter and enquiries of other growers who follow this practice tend to support my explanation. On much the same theme, careless use of a border fork or a dutch hoe can easily cause wounds to the crown and similar bleeding. Furthermore slugs, which can so easily destroy dormant eyes, also leave in their wake an open wound with the same result.

It is generally agreed that some cultivars seem to be more prone to rot and in this connection the actual hardness of the crown plays a part. Soft crowns, often found in darker coloured delphiniums, seem to be more susceptible while plants with hard crowns are more likely to survive for years. For my own part I am convinced that sensible cultivation, without the over-generous application of nitrogenous fertilizers leading to a forced lushness and softer crowns, will help considerably if coupled with careful cultivation of the soil around the plants.

It must also be said that the problem of rot is definitely linked to perenniality and some modern cultivars are perhaps introduced before they have been tested for a reasonable period of time. Perenniality is a quality very much sought after by Blackmore & Langdon Ltd, and many a fine plant has been withdrawn or not released by them because of the doubtful nature of its ability to survive undisturbed for many years. (Chapter 6 mentions which cultivars possess true perennial characteristics, but only take this as a rough guideline. Other cultivars may also prove to be long-lived with many growers.)

Soil Sickness

Although not strictly a disease in the true sense there appear to be indications, founded on the experience of growers of long-

1 'Sandpiper', a modern white cultivar, with black
   or brownish eyes, and a good example of the
   desirable pyramidal spike

2 A section of Blackmore & Langdon's stand at the Chelsea Flower Show

3 'Swan Lake', a typical example of columnar habit but a good garden plant, its black eye contrasting with white florets

4 Seedling raised by Dr D. Bassett.
   A very promising plant of heliotrope,
   selected for trial at Wisley

5 'Stardust', a good garden cultivar
6 A section of one of the Delphinium
   Society's shows

Delphiniums from seeds:

7 Cotyledon stage: in another two
to three weeks the first true
leaves will appear

8 Seedling at ideal stage for planting
in open ground. Note that the root
system has not reached the stage
of becoming pot-bound

9 The embryo spike: will it be a winner?

Staking:

10 An anchor tie – one cane per shoot. Possibly the best system for the extra-large exhibition spike

11 The normal method, allowing the spikes to sway. In very exposed situations a further loose tie will be made further up the triangle, as the plant grows

12 Caterpillar damage: most of the
   embryo spike has been consumed

13 *Tortix* moth larva – a rare enemy
   of the delphinium

Fasciation:

14 'Shepherd's crook'

15 'Whiskering'

16 'Double head'

17 'Bunching'

18 Roy Broan, a Vice-President of the
Delphinium Society, with his 'short
blues'. Note that there are at least
twenty spikes on the one plant

standing, that habitually to cultivate delphiniums in the same area, year after year, can lead to a build-up in the soil of micro organisms that are harmful to the plants. While there is no firm evidence of how many years will elapse before deterioration is likely to take place, it does seem that it is safe for at least ten years, and possibly even longer. As with all plants it is sensible to practise crop rotation and to give a delphinium bed a rest, say, every fourth or fifth year. There is no need to keep the bed fallow, however, and it can safely be used for a different flower or even for vegetables, if this is aesthetically possible.

There is an alternative if space is at a premium and that is to sterilize the whole of the planting area, in order to destroy eel worms, other harmful insects and debilitating bacteria. Great care will be needed, especially with some chemicals, as plants in close proximity may inadvertently be harmed in the process. Perhaps the safest sterilizing agent is cresylic acid, which is readily obtainable in practically any gardening shop, under a well-known proprietary name. While possibly not as effective as other, more modern sterilants, this chemical does have the advantage that it is unnecessary to cover the soil with plastic sheets afterwards, in order to trap the chemical effect for as long as possible.

There is always a chance of re-infecting soil which has been sterilized, but this is likely to be a gradual process. One way of minimizing re-infection is to propagate only from really healthy stock and to keep everything—tools, greenhouse, benches, pots, seed trays and perhaps, most important, your hands—absolutely clean and sterile. Guard against obtaining stock from doubtful sources and do remember that a possible source of infection is a gift of a cutting from a well-meaning friend whose garden hygiene leaves something to be desired. This happens all too easily, and more than once I have received the welcome gift of a desirable plant only to find a goodly supply of slug's eggs surrounding the crown.

Fasciation

Many perennial plants suffer from an abnormal growth condition, properly called fasciation, and the delphinium is no exception, but it is not generally a major problem (see Plates 14 to 17). In severe cases the flower spike can be distorted in a quite hideous manner, sometimes flattened or branching out into two spikes. A less chronic distortion is 'whiskering', when there is a complete absence of laterals: the whiskers are in reality misshapen leaves which are produced in hundreds and give the delphinium the appearance, in the early stages, of a bush.

The reason for fasciation in all its forms and in most plants is not well understood, and there are many theories. One suggestion, which is widely accepted, is indigestion caused by a sudden intake of plant food in times of lush growth. Another theory, which many consider accounts for fasciation, is late frosts when the plant is producing the embryo spike.

It must be said that the majority of named delphinium cultivars furnish, in all seasons, spikes free from this malady, giving rise to speculation that fasciation may be a genetic abnormality. But, whatever the cause, and although it can be irritating to find trouble of this nature, it should be kept in perspective. It affects only a tiny percentage of spikes and in most seasons it does not appear at all.

6 Cultivars Available Commercially

(E) Early; (M) Mid-Season; (L) Late Flowering;
(Ex) Recommended for Exhibition;
(S) Short; (A) Average Height; (T) Tall.

The usual practice of giving raiser's name, year of introduction and awards obtained has been omitted deliberately. Very full details of each cultivar listed, including up to date information as well as new introductions, can be obtained by reference to the register compiled by the Royal Horticultural Society or from the Delphinium Society.

'**Alice Artindale**' (E-A). One of the very few delphiniums with a fully double floret. The form is often referred to as 'ranunculus'. Bi-colour of rosy-mauve tinged with sky-blue. No eye. This cultivar was raised in 1935 and was popular as a commercial cut flower. There is evidence of marked deterioration in some strains and great care is needed with selection.

'**Anne Page** (E-A). An older cultivar once popular for exhibition but now superseded by superior cultivars. Cornflower-blue, blackish eye.

'**Antares**' (S). The deepest of the dusky pinks to receive an award after trial at Wisley.

'**Apollo**' (M-T). Large amethyst-purple florets, brown eye.

'**Baby Doll**' (M-S). Pale mauve, white eye.

'**Blue Dawn** (M-T). Sky-blue, flushed slightly with pink, small black eye.

Delphiniums

'Blue Jade' (M-S). Pastel blue, brown eye.

'Blue Nile' (M-A-Ex). Pure mid-blue with contrasting neat white eye. An excellent plant in every respect, longevity being but one of its virtures.

'Bruce' (M-T-Ex). Purple-violet with grey-brown eye.

'Butterball' (M-A-Ex). Deep cream, bright yellow eye, giving an overall appearance close to pale yellow.

'Cassius' (M-A). Purple, dark eye.

'Charles Gregory Broan' (M-S). Pale blue, white eye. An excellent garden plant.

'Celon' (M-T). Pale violet, white eye and large florets.

'Chelsea Star' (M-T-Ex). Rich velvety purple/deep violet, contrasting white eye. Large beautiful florets. Huge spikes. Prone to mildew.

'Cherub' (M-A). Pale pinkish-mauve, similar to 'Turkish Delight'.

'Cinderella' (M-S). Heliotrope-mauve, dark eye.

'Conspicuous' (M-A). Lilac-mauve, with a prominent brown eye.

'Cream Cracker' (M-A-Ex). The latest in the cream spectrum. Overall appearance yellowish. Vivid yellow eye. A fine vigorous cultivar. Stock scarce.

'Cristella' (E-A). Mid-blue, white eye. The earliest of the mid-blues.

'Crown Jewel' (M-A). Mid-blue, tinged slightly with pink tones, very large prominent black eye.

'Cupid' (M-S). Sky-blue, white eye. One of the shortest cultivars.

'**Daily Express**' (M-A). Sky-blue, rather untidy brownish eye. Rare colour, but losing some of its original vigour

'**Dolly Bird**' (M-A). Pale mauve, similar to 'Baby Doll' but taller.

'**Fanfare**' (E-T-Ex). Silvery pastel-mauve. A cultivar introduced many years ago, but still vigorous.

'**Faust**' (M-T). Ultramarine, with inconspicuous indigo eye. A good reliable garden plant.

'**Fenella**' (M-A-Ex). Gentian-blue, black eye. Introduced at almost the same time as 'Blue Nile'. A very reliable cultivar.

'**Garden Party**' (M-S). Pale dusty pink, white eye.

'**Gillian Dallas**' (L-A). Handsome slate blue-grey with a white eye. An endearing cultivar of beautiful form.

'**Gordon Forsyth**' (M-T-Ex). Pure amethyst, small dark eye. A fine shapely spike.

'**Guy Langdon**' (M/L-T-Ex). Plum-purple, striped eye. An outstanding exhibition cultivar. Inclined to drop bottom florets, especially when cut.

'**Gossamer**' (M-A-Ex). See 'Spindrift', to which it is similar. It is paler and also more regular in colour.

'**Harmony**' (M-A). Heliotrope, dark eye.

'**Hilda Lucas**' (L-T-Ex). Mainly blue, but tinged pinkish-mauve in back petals. An astonishing plant, extremely vigorous, long lived and robust. Produces enormously long graceful spikes and is probably the latest of all to bloom. A constant show winner.

'**Icecap**' (E-T-Ex). Pure white throughout; a fine, striking cultivar. Not a long-lived plant: requires renewing by cuttings every other year.

Delphiniums

'**Iona**' (M-A-Ex). White with black eye.

'**Judy Knight**' (M-A). A rare pale lavender-mauve, with contrasting eye.

'**Loch Katrine**' (E-S). Gentian-blue suffused purple with black eye.

'**Loch Leven**' (M-S-Ex). Light blue with white eye. A pretty delphinium of good constitution.

'**Loch Lomond**' (E-M-A). Rich blue with white eye.

'**Loch Maree**' (M-T-Ex). Rich blue with black eye.

'**Loch Morar**' (M-A). Rich blue with white eye.

'**Lock Ness**' (E-S). Genetian-blue, dark brown or black eye.

'**Loch Nevis**' (E-T-Ex). Light blue with white eye. Pyramidal spike of immense proportions—the most popular exhibition cultivar ever. Easy to grow well.

'**Loch Torridon**' (M-L-S-Ex). Light blue with white eye. Attractive plant of good constitution.

'**Lord Butler**' (M-S). Pale Cambridge-blue with white eye.

'**Marie Broan**' (M-A). Lavender-mauve with dark eye.

'**Michael Ayres**' (M-T). Rich violet with black eye.

'**Mighty Atom**' (L-S-Ex). Mid-violet, almost double in effect. Extremely vigorous.

'**Moonbeam**' (M-T-Ex). Entirely white throughout.

'**Morning Cloud**' (M-A). Pale blue, flushed slightly with pink, fawn eye.

'**Nimrod**' (M-T-Ex). Rich royal purple with small white eye. Tall and vigorous.

'**Olive Poppleton**' (M-T-Ex). A unique cultivar. Off-white with a large glowing honey-coloured eye. Strong growing.

'**Panda**' (M-A). White with black eye.

'**Pericles**' (M-A). Soft mid-blue with white eye.

'**Purple Ruffles**' (L-A-Ex). Almost fully double dark purple florets and wide pyramidal spikes. Rather prone to mildew, but a popular cultivar.

'**Rona**' (M-A-Ex). Greeny-white with white eye.

'**Rosina**' (M-A). Deep dusty pink with white eye.

'**Royal Flush**' (M-A-Ex). Perhaps the most vigorous of the dusky pinks. Large florets on long broad-based spikes. Shorter than most in this colour range.

'**Ruby**' (M-A). Deep mulberry-pink with brown eye on broad spike. A fine plant, vigorous.

'**Sabrina**' (E-S). A fine short cultivar, similar to 'Blue Nile', but a lighter blue. Good constitution.

'**Sabu**' (M-T-Ex). Darkest of the purples. Can produce huge spikes. Constitution not good, needs to be propagated annually to preserve the vigour. Prone to mildew.

'**Sandpiper**' (E-A-Ex). One of the best of the white cultivars, combining a contrasting black eye.

'**Savrola**' (M-T). Blue combined with plum-purple. A good strong grower.

'**Shimmer**' (L-T). Similar to 'Blue Nile', but taller and later.

'**Silver Jubilee**' (E-A). Shorter growing, white with black eye.

'**Sky Line**' (L-M). A lovely cultivar. Sky-blue with white eye. Of almost double appearance. Can be tricky to keep.

Delphiniums

'Spindrift' (M-A-Ex). A most unusual colour. It can produce in certain seasons and soils a definite turquoise effect with other colour combinations. Small white eye. High values for floral art.

'Strawberry Fair' (M-A-Ex). Mulberry-rose. Unusually strong stems for a dusky pink. Not the easiest to propagate.

'Summer Wine' (M-A-Ex). Mid-dusky pink with white eye.

'Sungleam' (M-A-Ex). Somewhat deeper in colour than 'Butterball'. Taller and of good constitution for this colour range.

'Swan Lake' (E-T). Clear white with black eye. The earliest of this type. Strong grower, but somewhat narrow spike.

'Thundercloud' (M-A). Deep purple with black eye. Good constitution.

'Tiddles' (M-A-Ex). Slate-mauve, no eye, producing an almost double floret. An attractive delphinium.

'Turkish Delight' (E-A-Ex). Pale dusky pink. Large clear florets with white eye. A fine cultivar of attractive form.

'Vespers' (M-A). Blue and mauve with white eye.

7 Delphiniums for the Garden

It is no longer necessary to limit delphiniums to the back of a border, as was common a few years ago, although they still have their place here in all but the smallest gardens. Facts have to be faced, however, and whether we like it or not, the plots on modern housing developments are forever shrinking in size. Happily, the choice of delphiniums suitable for mini-sized gardens is now wide and there are enough new cultivars of suitable dimensions in a large range of colours to have a representative display. Careful selection is vital, of course, for some of the exhibition cultivars would be entirely out of place in a narrow border.

Many of the short delphiniums now available grow to less than 4 ft (120 cm) tall and are generally more compact. The stems have a similar circumference to the taller plants and it is this sturdiness which makes them an ideal choice not only for the small garden, but also for planting in exposed situations known to suffer from summer gales. This new generation of tough plants requires a minimum of staking and more often than not can be grown without support in fairly sheltered areas. In many cases this shortness has been achieved without sacrificing the length of the bloom, for a significant proportion begin flowering as low as 12 in. (30 cm) from the soil and yet are still capable of producing flower spikes of 3 ft (90 cm) or more. Nor has the quality of the individual floret suffered: florets of between 3 and 4 in. (8 and 10 cm) across are commonplace and the colour range is as wide as in the taller plants.

Delphiniums

A number of enthusiasts have been captivated by these comparatively new short delphiniums as they can, if planted intelligently, make a wonderful impact, giving the impression of a solid wall of colour from ground level to 4-5 ft (120-150 cm). There is the added bonus that when the spikes are finally removed after flowering only 12 in. (30 cm) or so of stem is left, which is easily hidden if some thought has been given to the position they occupy and their association with other plants. The gardener can take advantage of every inch of space in a small garden if, for example, dahlias are planted in front of these smaller delphiniums: by mid to late July the dahlias will have made sufficient growth to hide completely those delphinium stems which must remain after flowering. There is a fine selection of perennial asters which can serve the same purpose, and also a wide range of colourful annuals. In fact the choice is only limited by the individual gardener's imagination.

For those who wish to maintain a predominance of the comparatively rare colour of blue in their gardens for as long as possible, there is the option of growing only delphiniums! By carefully selecting a dwarf delphinium seed strain and sowing under glass (as recommended in Chapter 2), the foliage will be sufficiently developed to hide completely the remains of the delphiniums which have bloomed at the normal time. Indeed, by setting out seedlings in front of their established plants, many growers are able to have delphinium spikes in bloom from mid June until November.

The taller cultivars are, of course, invaluable for the larger garden and also have their place in quite modest sized plots. You only need to see delphiniums in a rose garden to appreciate the wonderful contrast that these two plants make. It is a breathtaking sight to see bold plantings of the taller delphiniums against a background of climbing or rambling roses, blooming together during June and July. The contrasting hues of the roses act as a wonderful foil to the cooler colours of the delphinium and the differences in habit of growth seems to enhance the whole spectacle. It is small wonder that rose growers often develop a love of the delphinium and make extensive plantings of both; and many a delphinium enthusiast has also realized the potential of roses of all forms to complement his first love. No mixed border would be complete without bold groups of delphiniums and it is here that the taller plants have their special place, notably towards the rear. Again give consideration to the actual site, choosing wherever possible a position where a later blooming plant will hide the remains of the delphinium foliage after flowering.

It is far better to arrange all plantings of delphiniums so that groups of one cultivar are adjacent to each other, as the effect is far more rewarding than single plants dotted about. Colour too is important, and although very few delphiniums clash in colour with one other, it is always best to separate the true blues by, perhaps, a group of white. The various subtle shades obtainable in modern blue delphiniums can be lost if, for example, a pale sky-blue spike is seen next to a deep blue. Do not fall into the trap of placing all the tallest cultivars at the back of the border for, while it is true that a shorter plant should obviously be in front of its taller companion, it is better to try to achieve balance so that the effect is a graded one rather than a row of guardsmen-like spikes.

If the mixed border has a backing of a hedge or there are established shrubs, take care to plant delphiniums sufficiently far away to ensure that there is no competition for moisture. Failure to observe this aspect of siting is a frequent cause of poor spindly growth. A site in full sun is often held to be perfect for delphiniums and while this is reasonably logical some qualification is needed. There are some named plants which undoubtedly give of their best when grown in a fully open aspect and a classic example is 'Blue Nile'. This lovely cultivar is inclined to produce a rather loose spike when grown in even slighly shady conditions, whereas in full sun it will form a well-furnished bloom. On the other hand, 'Hilda Lucas' will benefit from a shady position, for the florets tend to overlap one another and this will be minimized as the spikes elongate and reach out towards the available light. The dusky pinks will also benefit considerably from a position where there is some shade from the full midday sun, as intense sunlight attacks the pigment in the florets with the result that they tend to bleach; shade will lessen this.

It pays, in fact, to grow delphiniums in various aspects in the garden for, by having some in a north-facing border and others in a sunnier south-facing site, the flowering season can be extended. There can be as much as two weeks' difference in the time of blooming in these two extremes which is not only desirable for full enjoyment, but can be a useful ally if the gardener has flower shows in mind.

As with many other flowers which have become popular for exhibitions there are some named plants that are more suitable for showing than for display in the garden—although there are, of course, many plants which are more than satisfactory for both purposes. There is no doubt, however, that some delphiniums require a great deal of attention in order to grow well in the garden and clearly they can be a nuisance.

'Sabu', for example, one of the darkest of the purples, can produce with expertise some staggeringly large spikes, often with 5 ft (150 cm) of bloom, but it is very prone to mildew and can look unsightly in the border if periodic steps are not taken to prevent disease. Moreover, it is not perennial and needs to be propagated annually to preserve, vigour. The same is true of some other cultivars, for example, 'Chelsea Star', 'Purple Triumph', 'Purple Ruffles' and 'Nimrod', and, unless you have competition in mind, these 'difficult' delphiniums are best left to those who are prepared to give that extra attention to detail required with these 'exhibitor's' plants.

Happily, the choice of delphiniums devoid of problems is large—'Blue Nile', 'Loch Nevis', 'Lock Leven' and 'Hilda Lucas' to name but four—and a good catalogue will indicate the virtues of all plants listed. Newly introduced named cultivars need to be selected cautiously. They are usually referred to as 'novelties' and sometimes fail to live up to expectations. Perhaps the finest insurance against buying an unsuitable delphinium is to restrict your choice to those plants which have received awards from the Joint Committee of the Royal Horticultural Society and the Delphinium Society (see Chapter 12). A comprehensive description is issued by the Trials Officer at the time when the award is made and includes not only the name of the raiser, but also the introducer, who is more often than not a commercial grower.

Regrettably there is nothing to prevent a raiser from naming a plant without registering it with the Royal Horticultural Society or sending it for trial so be suspicious of plants on sale which fall into this category. If in doubt it is wise to ask the nursery or garden centre for particulars of awards the plant has received and if the reply is negative then avoid these doubtful delphiniums. Insist on plants which have been tried and tested. The importance of this cannot be over-emphasized, for much disappointment will result from buying what are often extremely poor plants; and it is really relatively easy to choose delphiniums from a specialist grower that have received the highest accolade. Moreover, there is generally the added bonus that the seller is an expert, and an enthusiast who will be willing to recommend cultivars particularly suitable for your purposes.

In the normal way and in most seasons the bulk of delphiniums will bloom from mid June to mid July. The exhibitor would not dream of allowing his plants to bloom again the same year on the grounds that next year's display would suffer—he would, in fact, take steps to prevent this happening. For garden display, however, there is something to be said in

77

favour of getting as much colour in one year as the plant is capable of giving. Thus as soon as the flowers are past their best remove the main spike to allow the laterals to develop. A balanced feed should be given followed by copious supplies of water if rainfall has been sparse: the delphinium will respond to this treatment and you will be rewarded with a second blooming later in the year. In certain named cultivars, 'Daily Express' and 'Silver Jubilee', for example, laterals are not produced at all and in others they are fairly insignificant; these should be the plants which are cut down to ground level.

8 Delphiniums for Exhibitions

Much that has already been said about delphinium growing for garden display applies equally as well to the delphinium grown for exhibition. But there are some additional practices which will help produce those giant blooms 3-5 ft (90-150 cm) in length.

Perhaps too much emphasis has been placed on size by the keen exhibitor. Giant spikes are offensive to some eyes: they are said to be out of character and coarse in appearance, and there is some justification for this view. But a well-grown large spike can be a magnificent sight, especially with those cultivars that can stand an increase in size without loss of the ethereal quality which is almost exclusive to the delphinium.

There are certain cultivars which will never make a spike large enough to compete in normal classes at flower shows, and any attempt to force up large blooms will lead to a flower totally out of character. Make a note of successful cultivars at flower shows, especially those held in London. At the moment there are perhaps twenty consistent winners, so choose from the following if success is desired on the show bench: 'Bruce', 'Chelsea Star', 'Cream Cracker', 'Crown Jewel', 'Fanfare', 'Gillian Dallas', 'Gordon Forsythe', 'Guy Langdon', 'Hilda Lucas', 'Icecap', 'Loch Leven', 'Loch Nevis', 'Loch Torridon', 'Mighty Atom', 'Olive Poppleton', 'Sandpiper', 'Sabu', 'Spindrift', 'Strawberry Fair', 'Turkish Delight'.

This emphasis on size has caused concern for some years among the officers of the Dephinium Society, for many lovely cultivars were never seen at the shows in London simply because they were not of exhibition quality. To rectify this unfortunate omission, a new class was introduced by the Society in 1978 to celebrate its Golden Jubilee, thus enabling the public to see the wide range of colour and form available. Calling for spikes of a restricted size the success of this venture was such that more blooms were staged in this section than in any other class. It is to be hoped that other Societies will follow this lead. The would-be exhibitor should be aware of this recent change of emphasis and not merely have a collection of the larger types, although they still have an important role to play in national competitions.

Cultural Requirements

Exhibition delphiniums should be given a more generous planting space than those grown for the garden. A distance of 30 in. (75 cm) each way is sufficient for ease of cultivation and at the same time allows the root system of each plant enough soil area so that there is no competition for plant foods and moisture.

The single most important contribution a grower can make towards achieving sheer size is adequate thinning and it is more vital than any other cultural requirement. A well-grown one-year plant should not be allowed to carry more than two spikes and even a mature plant is not capable of producing more than four or five of exhibition quality for classes of unrestricted size. It is dangerous, however, to do this thinning in a single operation, because it may lead to a form of plant 'indigestion'. There is evidence (perhaps not conclusive) that the sudden upsurge of plant food to the few remaining stems after drastic thinning may cause fasciation, when the spike becomes distorted. So, to be on the safe side, do your thinning over several weeks.

It will also be necessary to feed your exhibition plants. Early in the year, say in March, give them nitrogen, which is most essential for vegetative growth, before the embryo spike is formed. Phosphates, while good for root structure, need not be applied for most soils have an adequate supply as the chemical residues are not leached from the soil in the same way as nitrogen. Potash is important in the production of large spikes and it should be applied at least six weeks before flowering for the effects to be of any use. Later applications will not become available to the plant until after flowering. This ingredient not only enhances the colour of the florets, but also hardens the stems so that they are able to withstand the effects of gales to a much greater degree. It is not possible to give the exact quantities required for so much depends on the fertility of your soil and the chemicals used. The advice so often given can only be repeated: **read the instructions and obey them to the letter**. Giving a bit more for luck is a waste and indeed can do harm.

All this industry will be to little avail in raising a winner for the show bench if the plants are allowed to suffer through lack of moisture. Even though it may be hard to believe, we seldom receive enough rainfall in the United Kingdom constantly to supply the shallow roots of the delphinium: it is a plant that needs ample moisture. Recourse to watering is inevitable and a good soaking must be given during periods of little or no rain. Do not be put off or worry when your neighbours give you odd looks for putting the sprinkler on your delphiniums when it is raining. A light shower in May is no doubt useful for seed in the vegetable plot, but it is of little help in the delphinium bed.

There are no secret potions or formulas for success. It is really a matter of treating your delphiniums in much the same way as you would a successful vegetable garden—where a fertile soil, thinning, and feeding and watering lead to bumper crops.

Showing

There are a number of artifices which exhibitors of other flowers use in order to preserve their selected blooms in show condition for as long as possible. Rose growers tie the blooms together and use refrigerators; gladiolus fanciers use dark cupboards and variations in temperature. Exercises such as these are not possible with delphiniums in view of their size and also because the average show spike will have upwards of fifty individual florets fully open. Happily, there is no need for recourse to these somewhat doubtful practices, for the delphinium will remain in show condition for several days, and even for as long as a week in cool conditions.

Selection of delphiniums. Submission of entry forms for the national shows and those taking place in large towns is usually required one week in advance. Beginners sometimes find it difficult to estimate at this early stage the likelihood of their spikes being in pristine condition at the right time. Fortunately, there are several useful guidelines which enable the exhibitor to complete the form with reasonable confidence. In normal circumstances it takes roughly three weeks from the time the embryo is first observed to maturity. Moreover, when the lowest floret has opened it will take around five days for it to be half out and a further five days or so for the bloom to be fully developed. Armed with this information it is fairly easy to select those delphiniums which are likely to be good candidates.

It is quite satisfactory to stage a flower which is not fully developed and very often prizewinners are selected by judges when only three-quarters open, for freshness is of prime importance. The Delphinium Society have recommended that a spike should be open as far as possible, but not at the expense of dropping florets; stripped stems or florets showing seed pods will be deemed serious defects.

Overall appearance. Another important consideration to bear in mind is the overall appearance of the delphinium. Judges like to see florets so distributed that the finished effect is that of a well-furnished but not overcrowded spike, and the length should be dependent on the character of the flower. Avoid selecting those spikes which are inclined to be gappy or ones where each floret overlaps its neighbour.

Florets. Recommendations for these are less easy to define. Individual florets should be fully open and of uniform character throughout the spike. Sepals must be firm and of good substance, with regular and neat eyes. Judges are not impressed by florets which are cupped or those giving an asymmetrical appearance. Avoid cultivars or your own seedlings which produce very thin petals and instead try to pick those with an almost waxy look about them.

Eyes can have a tremendous impact on the look of a floret and substantial ones of a contrasting nature always have a pleasing effect. Avoid those delphiniums where the eye is untidy or ragged-looking and particularly where the colour has 'spilled over' into the inner petals, as sometimes happens.

Colour. This has the least influence on judges as it is recognized to be so much a question of personal preference. It can, however, be important if the judges are faced with two spikes of equal merit: the one which is cleanest in colour will generally sway the final decision.

Laterals. Because of the difficulty of transporting delphiniums to shows, a previous rule regarding the staging of spikes with at least three laterals attached has now been dropped. No differentiation will be made between those shown with or without laterals.

There are often separate classes for laterals and in general the same guidelines apply, but with the additional recommendation that stems should have sufficient substance to carry the weight of the florets.

Classes for individual florets. These classes in national shows call for six florets in each entry. In addition to the remarks already made, the judges will be looking for uniformity of size, clearness and range of colour and, lastly, presentation.

Preparation for showing. It is best to cut the spike of your choice with a sharp knife as secateurs tend to crush. A good plan is to fill the hollow stem with water and plug the end with cotton-wool to help preserve freshness. Have an eye to weather forecasts as there is really little point in trying to transport a spike which is wet, for it will not be fit for exhibiting by the time you arrive at the show. There are many successful exhibitors who cut their spikes the day before and put them in deep vases under cover until they are needed.

Always take advantage, where it is possible, to stage on the penultimate day for it is by far the most satisfactory way, giving the blooms sufficient time to recover from the inevitable crushing which takes place on their journey to the show. Most of us have cars these days and an estate type has obvious advantages, but whatever transport you use tissue paper helps to separate the spikes. A useful tip for those using public transport is to obtain the cardboard boxes in which manufacturers pack fluorescent light tubes as these are sturdily made and will accommodate at least four spikes; again each one should be separated by a layer of tissue paper.

On arrival at the show place your delphiniums in water immediately, and only then have a look around to find your cards and positions on the benches. The preparation of each spike for the vases is of the utmost importance, for the delphinium blooms at the warmest time of the year and in late

June or early July a show can often occur during a heat-wave. The exhibitor should aim to keep his entries as fresh and turgid as possible, and there are three methods which are widely practised by seasoned showmen, each one being regarded by its devotees as *the* panacea. Unfortunately there is no evidence to suggest that any one method gets better results than the others; I suspect they all have similar effects! I can but describe each in turn and leave the reader to form his own opinion. All three have in common the making of a fresh oblique cut at the bottom of the stem.

Perhaps the most popular procedure is to make this fresh slanting cut, with a sharp knife, and then fill the stem with water again, taking care to prevent an air-lock. This is easy to avoid: simply let the water trickle in from the spout of a small can, such as those decorative utensils available or watering pot plants in the home. Now we come to the tricky part which requires a certain knack, and confidence. With the thumb firmly in place over the cut end right the spike from its inverted position and insert it, with the thumb still in position, into the water. The theory is that capillary action will continue to draw the water up the stem—which would not be the case if air was present in the hollow stem.

The second method is very similar, and is used a great deal by flower arrangers; they call it 'conditioning'. After the fresh cut is made, again with a knife, the stem is filled with water and then plugged with cotton wool before the spike is arranged in the vase.

Finally, and easiest of all, the oblique cut is made under water with secateurs. Using secateurs in this instance is fine, because any fracture or crushing takes place under water, and those who favour this method argue that the water is drawn up, not into the hollow stem but by the plant tissues in the wall of the spike. A possible air-lock is thus prevented which could stop the flow of water through the plant tissues.

Whatever method is adopted, though, take one spike at a time and make sure that you cut the stem so that the spikes conform to the standards of uniformity set by the Delphinium Society. A spike, say, 2 ft (60 cm) in length, for example, would not present a satisfactory appearance if 8 in. (20 cm) or more of stem was visible above the top of the vase, whereas the extra stem in a spike of twice this length would be in keeping with the size of the bloom. Always try to make the cut so that the amount of stem between the bottom floret and the top of the vase is in proportion to the length of the spike.

Paper is often used to pack around the stem, to keep the delphinium upright in its vase, but this is not usually satisfactory. It can easily lead, several hours later, to a spike falling out of the perpendicular with the danger of the whole vase toppling over. It is far better to bring some pieces of stem with you and cut them in suitable lengths for packing out the container. Sometimes the top of the vase can look rather untidy, but placing individual delphinium leaves around the stems can improve the overall appearance of your exhibit and is to be recommended for its aesthetic value alone.

The seasoned exhibitor will often have a final look around and may even have taken spare blooms with him. He will be looking for weaknesses in his own exhibits compared with other entries. He may, for example, decide to swop spikes from one class to another in the hope that he may strengthen one of his entries at the deliberate expense of another, in which he feels he has little chance of an award. This is all part of the hustle and bustle of flower shows and is often the cause for much merriment and good-natured leg pulling by fellow competitors.

A novice can learn much by just 'having a go'. In fact it is really the best method of learning how to exhibit, and it also gives the beginner the chance to question the old hand, who will usually be more than willing to pass on the tips he has acquired through years of experience.

9 Delphiniums for Vases and Containers

In 1958 the Delphinium Society published a booklet entitled 'Delphiniums are versatile', and this title is still most appropriate. Apart from its beauty as a garden flower and its successes in exhibitions, the delphinium can be used superbly by flower arrangers and, grown in tubs or containers, is a valuable addition to the small patio gardens which are becoming ever more popular.

Delphiniums for Flower Arrangements

The large exhibition-type spikes are clearly of little value in all but the largest of homes. I do, however, recall some spectacular arrangements in churches when main spikes were used to occupy a space some 6 ft (1.8 m) square. I have also seen a superb display in the reception area of a famous London hospital and in this case the lady arranger was clearly overjoyed to have the challenge of dealing with some thirty main spikes of a size she had not handled before. The result was quite breathtaking and, being the supplier, I was deeply gratified to witness the way in which medical staff, visitors and patients were literally stopped in their tracks when they caught sight of the sheer dignified gracefulness of this composition of delphiniums.

Of course, main spikes need not be the giants of the exhibition hall: a mature plant is capable of producing as many as thirty spikes nearer to 2 ft (60 cm) in length. These smaller

87

blooms can be used very effectively in even a modest sized home and can be displayed to advantage, for example, in the hearth of a fireplace. They really give of their best as a pedestal arrangement, for the spikes may then be placed at almost any angle; they look particularly beautiful in an entrance hall.

But it is the laterals or side shoots which perhaps find most favour in the small compact homes of today—and the possible flower arrangements with them are endless. If this is the type of growth which appeals, then do make your selection of plants very carefully indeed. Some cultivars hardly produce a lateral while others are generous in this respect; and in some the laterals are very tiny and almost useless except for the really small vase.

For a white delphinium it is hard to find a more productive lateral-bearing plant than 'Swan Lake'. Indeed, with this cultivar, an umbrella of some thirty or more laterals will result if the main spike is pinched out as soon as it is visible. You may have to hunt around for this delphinium for it is not listed by many nurserymen. In the blue range 'Loch Leven', a short growing cultivar, produces excellent laterals, whereas 'Loch Nevis', for example, a grand plant for arrangers as it seldom drops its florets, has few side shoots and these are invariably very small in length. The choice is wide in the purple range, but steer clear of 'Guy Langdon' for not only does it have few laterals, it also sheds its petals soon after cutting.

The safest way of selecting the best delphiniums for flower arrangements is to visit a comprehensive display in a garden or nursery during mid July, when laterals will be in full production. Close examination will reveal which plants tend to have poor holding qualities—especially important today, as much thought has been given to this aspect by recent raisers. There are now several newish cultivars which are noted for their ability to 'hold' the bottom florets until the top ones are open.

On many modern cultivars, particularly those of a pyramidal

shape, an individual floret may be born on a pedicel measuring as much as 9 in. (23 cm). These lend themselves well to posy arrangements and if removed from the side of a spike, facing away from the normal view of the border, then there will be no need to cut an entire spike. Individual florets also make exceptionally fine button-holes and if backed by an immature leaf they are a splendid alternative to the more traditional carnation used at weddings.

Drying Delphiniums

The moisture content of laterals is not as high as in the main spikes, so they are a far better proposition for drying for winter decoration. Both will, however, keep their colour far better than most other hardy perennials. (A dried specimen of *D. orientale* was found in the tomb of King Ahmes I: it still retained its colour, from 1700 BC.)

It is important to select immature laterals, that is to say, specimens where only about half the florets are opened. Try to avoid cutting laterals during a warm period: cut them in the cool of the evening, and place them overnight in a tall container filled with a mixture of half water and half glycerine. In the morning remove the laterals and hang them upside down in a place where there is no dampness and no direct sunlight. By choosing such a site, rotting will be avoided and the colours will not be bleached. After approximately a week, in average conditions, the florets will feel dry and yet somewhat silky to the touch. Now is the time to place them loosely in a cardboard box and store them in a cool, dry place until they are required.

Delphiniums in Tubs or Containers

Any visitor to the Chelsea Flower Show will confirm that superb delphiniums can be grown in large pots. Each year without fail Blackmore & Langdon produce a breathtaking display of superb spikes for their stand, grown in containers. Of course, the object of the exercise in their case is to steal a march on the weather by producing delphiniums, under glass, some four to six weeks before their normal flowering period. But it does indicate that delphiniums are perfectly at home in tubs.

Why, one may ask, grow them in containers anyway? The answer to this question is a topical one for there is an awakening interest in patios, so suitable for the mini-sized plots which are the general rule in today's building developments. Perhaps a word is needed about the management of such areas, for the secret of decorating a patio is limiting permanent plantings, in order to have room for a selection of plants in pots or containers. Delphiniums are admirable subjects for this purpose, grown and brought to near maturity in a 'nursery area' in some odd corner of the garden, often sited behind screens of stone or trellis erected to furnish the patio area with a boundary and to provide privacy as well as a suitable background to the containerized plants. Obtain young rooted delphinium cuttings, still growing in their small pots, in the late spring or early summer—never purchase mature plants as they will lead to disappointment or even complete failure—and keep them in suitable tubs or containers in the nursery area until they are about to flower.

Cheap and practical containers are readily obtainable from horticultural sundriesmen in the form of large pots made from a dark green plastic with a ribbed moulding to the sides and a lip turned outwards to provide a firm support when the pots are lifted. Choose ones that are approximately 12 in. (30 cm) in diameter, but the most important point to look for is the flexibility of these tubs. Those constructed of a soft and not brittle plastic are best, otherwise fractures may easily occur when they are moved from place to place.

Make generous drainage holes in the base of these plastic

pots, either by using a drill or a heated piece of metal. Then place 1 in. (2.5 cm) of wet peat in the bottom and follow this with a compost, preferably of the John Innes type, which has been prepared for 'potting-on'. Do not make the mistake of filling the tub to the brim, but leave about 2 in. (5 cm) of space for the liberal applications of water that will be necessary from time to time. Please do make certain that the compost is really firm, for loose planting is a frequent cause of poor flowering.

Plant the young rooted cuttings about ½ in. (1.25 cm) deeper than the original soil level, one cutting per container, and water in well. See that the plant does not suffer through lack of moisture during the summer and remember it is almost impossible to kill a delphinium by over-watering, providing there is adequate drainage. During this period the plant will be more than happy with a shady position; in fact this can be an advantage as the pot will not dry out so readily. By the late summer, or even earlier in favourable locations, there will be the unmistakable evidence of the plant showing its willingness to flower. Encourage it to produce blooms by adding to the waterings a liquid fertilizer which contains the more important trace elements as well as the usual proportion of nitrogen, phosphate and potash. You will be rewarded with at least one spike in the first year, blooming in the late summer or early autumn, and it is when the first floret begins to show colour that the tub can be brought on to your patio and given a minimum of staking behind the spike.

When the bloom has faded return the tub to its former nursery site and remove the spent spike, taking great care to leave all foliage intact. As with naturally grown plants the foliage will gradually wither and die down during the autumn and early winter. The only treatment until the following spring is the scattering of a few slug pellets on the surface of the container and perhaps occasional watering in really dry spells.

With the advent of spring the following year fresh growth will

91

appear and with most cultivars the number of shoots will be far too many for the plant to sustain in its unnatural environment. Leave two at the most, unless the plant is exceptionally vigorous, in which case three shoots should be regarded as the absolute maximum. Thinning should be undertaken in a manner precisely similar to that mentioned in Chapter 8.

You can use the surplus shoots for propagation at this stage, and to this end there is a very useful tip. Prepare another container, as already described, and insert a cutting into a depression made in the centre of the surface, to which a handful of coarse grit has been placed. Firm the unrooted cutting well and put an inverted jam jar over it so that the rim of the jar rests on the soil. Make sure the tub is sited well away from the direct rays of the sun and in a matter of four to six weeks the cutting will have rooted direct into its permanent home and the jam jar should then be removed. Rapid growth will occur by using this method for there will be no disturbance caused by transplanting and a very vigorous plant will be the result.

Having thinned your one-year-old delphinium in its tub, be sure not to starve it. Most of the plant foods will have been exhausted in the past twelve months and these must be replaced. The simplest method is to give a weak liquid feed each time the plant is watered and it is a good plan to add a systemic insecticide during early spring, as a measure against the slight chance of a caterpillar attack. Again, later in the summer, an addition of a systemic fungicide can be useful in combating mildew, if you have selected a cultivar known to be susceptible to this disease. Unlike a delphinium growing in the open ground, a plant in a tub should be discarded after the second year and a fresh start made with a young cutting, which is, after all, a simple process. Vigour will be maintained by this method, whereas there will be a marked deterioration of a tub-grown plant if kept for a third year.

You can also raise delphiniums out of season, by using a

greenhouse, to produce a bloom at least a month earlier. Of course, it is only sensible to choose the shorter growing plants, unless you have a larger structure than normal. By careful management, as practised by the trade, it is possible to time the actual blooming fairly accurately simply by removing the tub from the greenhouse in times of excessive heat or returning it if the plant appears to be backward. But do be watchful, for growth and development can be alarmingly speedy during warm weather in the balmy environment of a glasshouse.

It is astonishing how well a delphinium will grow in the comparatively small amount of soil available in a tub. It is possible to produce several spikes of almost exhibition quality and certainly they offer the exciting prospect of an unusual and eye-catching addition to the normal range of patio plants.

10 Improving Your Delphiniums

Many gardeners who have grown the best named delphiniums for a number of years and have, as a result, become thoroughly familiar with the finer points of assessing a quality bloom develop a desire to improve their plants, be it their colour, form, lasting qualities or indeed any other aspect which appeals.

A Mini-trial of Delphiniums

It needs only a little space to conduct a trial of delphiniums from seed and I can promise anyone with the slightest interest in gardening the thrill of a lifetime when the first floret unfurls. Many of the blooms will be inferior to named cultivars; some will be almost as good; and there is always the chance of raising a 'winner'. Whatever the results, there is nothing quite like inspecting your own trial each day, usually first thing in the morning, as the fever grips to see yet another spike beginning to show colour.

For trial purposes only a relatively small patch of ground is required. As an example, a plot some 10 × 3ft (3 × 1 m) will accommodate fifty seedlings 9 in. (23 cm) apart each way. This is adequate spacing for our purposes, but make certain that the soil has been enriched in order to cope with such intensive cultivation by adding a general fertilizer to the patch at the highest rate recommended a week or so before planting out your young seedlings. Plants from 3 in. (7.5 cm) pots are preferable to those taken straight from a tray, for there will obviously be less root disturbance.

Once planted out delphiniums should never lack moisture, and be sure to add a high nitrogenous fertilizer as the plants begin to grow. Recourse to watering will almost certainly be required from time to time: be generous, so that the water penetrates deeply, because your aim should be to produce lush, vigorous growth. Delphiniums respond magnificently to a rich diet.

If you planted them in early to mid-spring, your seedlings should make a tremendous surge of growth as June approaches, and you will notice the first signs of a bloom on the most forward plants. As that month ends the seedlings will be showing their anxiety to bloom by starting to run-up. It is a strange fact that this intensive cultivation almost invariably encourages the plants to produce only one spike, and this will be of quite a representative size, since all your efforts have been to persuade the lone spike to receive a prodigious diet of food and water. Staking can be minimal as the close planting tends to support one spike against another.

Selection

If you have never experienced the excitement of growing a recommended mixed strain of delphiniums your hardest task is yet to come. It is most unlikely that any of your trial seedlings will resemble one another. Some of their differences will be obvious, such as colour or height. Others differences will be quite subtle, but it will not take you long to observe these. What you must do is to harden your heart and remove the entire plant if it does not reach a certain standard. What are these standards? Well, most of them will become obvious as you admire your mini-trial.

Colour is obviously one, but as this is so much a question of

Vegetative propagation – eye cuttings:

19 A typical eye being removed close to the crown, by an extremely keen blade

20 Eye after cutting

Vegetative propagation – orthodox cuttings:

21 Thinning plant and at the same time taking some useful cuttings

22 One operation – two end products. A one-year-old plant, thinned to two shoots and three cuttings obtained in the process

23 Plant lifted in early spring to facilitate removal of cuttings. Note how
    close the cut is made to the crown

24 A typical cutting, prepared by removing the lower leaves and ready for
    placing in the rooting medium
25 The good and the bad. The left hand base shows the beginnings of hollowness,
    the right hand is solid

Rooting cuttings:

26 Window sill propagation. One cutting per jar; note the fine root system

27 Silva Perllite can produce a very fine root system

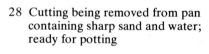

28 Cutting being removed from pan containing sharp sand and water; ready for potting

29 A well-grown cutting. Note new
    base growth which has appeared after
    the main growing point of the original
    cutting was removed

30 The perfect rooted cutting, ready
    for planting out

Hybridization:

31 Florets closed. A trifle early
   for emasculation

32 The ideal stage: the floret can be
   teased open gently for emasculation

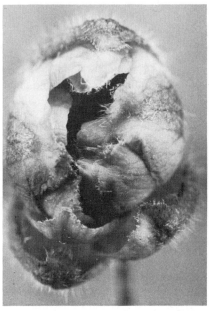

33 Floret unprepared

34 Emasculated floret

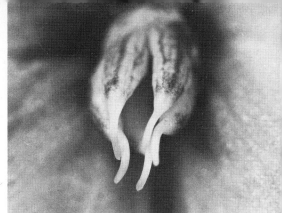

35 Stigma and style immediately
after emasculation

36 Male parent with a plentiful supply
of pollen, ready for transferring
to a receptive stigma

37 A cross is made: ripe pollen being
applied to a receptive stigma

38 A successful cross: fine fat seed
pods ready for harvesting

39 Dr Bob Legro and the author in the research glasshouses at the Wageningen University in the Netherlands

personal choice I do not propose to make any recommendations. A serious fault is weakness of stem: it is pointless keeping a plant where the spikes fracture in summer storms. Be on the look-out, too, for spikes which are not yet fully open but are dropping their bottom florets; these should be ruthlessly discarded. Somewhat more controversial is form. The perfectionist would look askance at a gappy spike or one with a blunt top. Irregular placement of florets offends the eye and I would discard plants with this fault. One fault not readily apparent concerns the eye or bee of the plant. Sometimes the colour of this part of the flower will tend to smudge into the central petals of the floret, giving an untidy look. The florets can be arranged on the stem in such a manner that they droop downwards or even upwards: these too are faults and are known as 'shy' or 'proud' blemishes.

If you find that you have a really superb seedling, resist the temptation to remove the plant to a more favourable spot. Leave it *in situ* so that full vigour may be maintained until you are able to propagate it vegetatively the following year.

Hybridization

We noted the hybrid nature of the delphinium in Chapter 1, where we saw that most of the improvements which have taken place are the result of deliberately crossing different cultivars. Natural mutation is so rare that the chances of any further changes taking place through this phenomena are extremely slight; progress will come mainly through hybridization.

Your chances of raising a real 'winner' will be increased considerably if you sow seeds obtained from a deliberate hand-cross between two cultivars. Fortunately the art of crossing one named cultivar with a different named cultivar is quite simple and can easily be achieved by anyone with a few minutes a day to spare.

Before discussion how to make a cross it is necessary to understand how nature attends to this process. The matter is somewhat controversial, but all authorities agree that the majority of hardy perennial delphiniums will set seed with their own pollen, that is to say, they are self-fertile. What is not generally accepted is the role played by insects and, in particular, the honey bee, in cross-pollination.

I am confident that insects or bees only play at best an insignificant part in transferring pollen from one delphinium to another. My own observation, since I became intrigued with this subject, is that honey bees are not over-fond of the nectar in a delphinium floret, for they are not frequent visitors. On genial days in mid-summer, when the air is full of their buzzings, I have observed my delphiniums closely and noted that the bees are conspicuous by their absence.

Furthermore, it is a generally accepted fact that the pollen from a delphinium floret is in viable condition somewhat before the stigma is receptive. The pollen has, therefore, already been scattered on the surface of the floret and it needs only the merest trace of movement, caused by a gentle breeze, to shake the pollen onto the glutinous stigma. Once this has taken place the effect of an insect bearing pollen on its body would be nil, for the selfed cross will have already occurred.

As an admittedly rather unscientific experiment in 1978 I placed a nylon stocking over an immature spike long before any floret was opened. The end of the stocking was securely bound with adhesive tape to prevent the entry of insects. Some six weeks later the stocking was removed and each and every floret had produced seed pods, all of which were filled in time with an average quota of viable seed, as germination tests later proved.

On another spike I emasculated ten florets by taking away their anthers, and removed the remainder. Not one of these florets yielded seed. It could, of course, be argued that an insect or bee would not visit a flower which could not produce pollen, and so this was an inconclusive experiment. Had there been any seed, however, it would have tended to support those who consider that insects or bees play an important role in cross-fertilization.

I hope that by narrating these two minor experiments the would-be hybridist will more readily understand the necessary steps required to achieve a cross—even if the conclusions I have reached are not accepted by all fellow enthusiasts.

The first requirement when making a cross is to prevent the seed-bearing parent from producing pollen with which it would otherwise fertilize itself. It is essential, therefore, to choose an immature floret at the stage before it begins to unfurl (but not when it is in tight bud or damage may occur). It is a simple matter, using the thumb and forefinger, gently to tease the floret open. This will reveal the immature anthers to the naked eye: it is this part of the flower which produces the pollen and it must be prevented from doing so, otherwise self-fertilization will take place and a cross will not be possible. Fortunately, the anthers can be removed at this early stage without damaging the rest of the seed-producing part of the floret. The stigma, which is the receptive portion, will not be visible to the naked eye at this stage (see Plate 33).

For those with good eyesight it is possible to detach the anthers, using the nails of the thumb and forefinger in a pinching action and giving a sharp twist and a pull. It must be admitted that this requires a certain amount of confidence, but there is an alternative: a cheap watchmaker's eyeglass plus a pair of tweezers will facilitate the easy removal of the anthers one at a time. It would appear that this action stimulates the growth of the stigma. In average temperatures it will become receptive in about four days by exuding a sticky substance.

It is at this stage that we should examine carefully the other cultivar chosen, to ensure that there is a plentiful supply of fresh pollen on the anthers, which can easily be detected by the naked eye (see Plate 36). If there is, remove the entire floret and fold the petals back. It becomes an easy matter to dab the exposed pollen-bearing anthers gently onto the receptive stigma: the pollen will adhere with every expectation of a successful union. If conditions have been cool it is possible that the union may not have taken place. As a safeguard, repeat the process again a day or two later and you will usually hit upon a time when the stigma has reached full maturity.

In the majority of cases the procedure I have outlined will be sufficient to achieve the desired cross. The fertilized floret will, in time, produce seed which should be harvested just before the pods turn a deep brown colour (see Plate 38). A certain indication of the failure of a cross is the twisting of the seed capsules, for on examination these pods will be found to be empty.

There are times, however, when a more sophisticated method may be used, particularly when the seed-bearing and the pollen-bearing parents are not ready at the same time. Pollen may be collected from the anthers over a period of several days and stored in a small glass phial (a plastic pill box is ideal). Simply insert the anthers into the neck of the vessel and give the floret a sharp tap. The pollen will remain in a viable condition in a domestic refrigerator for a considerable time, and certainly long enough for transfer by a soft artist's brush to the seed-bearing parent. This method is particularly useful when weather conditions are poor or when you want to achieve a cross between an early and a late cultivar.

Breeding with a Purpose in Mind

Haphazard breeding is not going to get you far, although it must be said that results from even casual crossing will generally produce a better range of seedlings than selfed seed. Many of the latter will bear characteristics similar, if not desirable, to the parents.

Unfortunately, it is little use trying to ascertain the parentage of a particular cultivar. In almost all cases the pedigree of named delphiniums is obscure, for more often than not several unknown seedlings have been used over many generations in the breeding process to arrive at a successful named plant. This multi-hybrid quality is something that the breeder has to live with so far as delphiniums are concerned. The best course of action is to ignore the history of cultivars and proceed on a line breeding course using your own promising seedlings. This approach has been used very effectively in recent years by amateurs.

How do you begin such a series of deliberate crosses with some real purpose in mind? The mini-trial, which was described at the beginning of this chapter, provides a most useful starting point. It will almost certainly be possible to select several plants from the trial which are of pleasing appearance yet may have a fault or indeed faults. Supposing, for example, one plant has the colour desired, but is spoilt by thinness of spike. It may be that another favoured seedling has a superb shape to the spike and in all other respects is a fine plant, but is marred by an undesirable colour combination. By crossing these two plants both ways—that is to say by using one seedling first as the seed-bearer and the other as the pollen-parent and then by reversing the roles—a dual cross will have been achieved. One hopes that by this action the virtues of one plant will have been passed to the other, and again, vice versa.

A careful record should be kept otherwise you will soon be in a hopeless muddle as continued crosses take place with the progeny year by year. The easiest method is a 'stud book', using a form of code.

You may, of course, be disappointed with your results and succeed in absolutely nothing by way of improvement. This is inevitable and the solution is to begin again with an entirely different parent. Any seedlings from the first cross which show improvement, however slight, are cause for optimism and you may consider it desirable to 'back cross' onto one or both of the original parents. The combination of crosses possible is endless and the permutations vast—so beware of failure to label and record details.

One factor which may register with you after a time is the ability of one of your parent plants to pass on a particular characteristic each time a cross is made. This is known as a dominant feature and often occurs in delphiniums. On the other hand recessive characteristics are also common. Being aware of both these facets can be a useful ally and can provide certain short cuts in breeding.

These then are the 'bare bones' of this fascinating and exciting branch of delphinium culture. I hope that enough has been said to start the enthusiast on the right path to producing a delphinium of sufficient quality to be selected for trial at the Royal Horticultural Society's gardens at Wisley. There is no easy road, and patience and luck are required. But if this were not so there would be no challenge and the development of the delphinium would come to an end.

11 A Delphinium Calendar

January

If you have done the work recommended for the autumn months, then this is the one month of the year when it is possible to 'rest on your laurels'—unless you are a real enthusiast and have the advantage of a greenhouse with some form of heat. If mature crowns are lifted now and replanted in the warmth of a gently heated greenhouse, new growth will occur within a few weeks and cuttings may be taken as much as two months sooner than from plants still in the open ground. Rooting will occur two months earlier too, with obvious benefits.

Seed may also be sown under glass during January with even a very modest amount of heat. A temperature of 50-60°F (10-15°C) is required, which is easily and cheaply achieved by the use of a small propagator or by placing the seed tray over the source of heat used to keep the frost out. These sowings, if properly cared for, are capable of producing exceedingly fine spikes by summer. A whole year can thus be saved because a proper selection can be made at the time of flowering, whereas later sowings will in all probability have to be left for a further year in order to make an objective assessment.

February

Seedlings from a sowing made the previous autumn and left in their original seed tray will usually have started into growth by now. It is an advantage to pot these up individually into 3 in.

Delphiniums

(7.5 cm) pots, which can remain outside until they are large enough for planting out. Further batches of seed may be sown under glass and cuttings taken from crowns placed under glass. In a mild season the first cuttings may also be available from open ground plants.

Slugs not dealt with the previous autumn should be ruthlessly exterminated now. The worst offender at this time of the year is the slug which mostly remains below soil level. A watering of a solution of aluminium sulphate at the rate of 1½ oz (40 g) to the gallon is the best method of attack. Avoid splashing foliage with this chemical because of its somewhat caustic effect.

March

Autumn-sown seedlings will be sufficiently developed to be planted in their trial ground. March is the main month in which to take cuttings from plants grown in the open ground. It is a good plan to tidy up the soil and remove all weeds during this operation. If the soil is poor, perhaps due to inadequate preparation, it is also an advantage to dress it with a balanced fertilizer at the same time, choosing for preference an organic-based brand as the effects are usually much longer lasting.

Seedlings from a January sowing will need to be transplanted into more spacious accommodation, ideally into 3 in. (7.5 cm) pots, though a deep tray will serve nearly as well. Cuttings which are being rooted in a cold frame need to be protected from strong sunshine and some shading will be necessary. Water cuttings, on the other hand, seem to tolerate extra heat well, but even here some shading is an advantage to prevent the water drying out.

April

Continue to take cuttings from late-appearing cultivars and pot them when rooted. If caterpillars are troublesome it is a good plan to give the plants a spray of a systemic insecticide to prevent damage occurring. Pinch out the growing point of those rooted cuttings which were potted up in March, in order to stimulate breaks of new growth from the base. Order any new cultivars without delay so as to catch the normal delivery time which is from May to June. Popular and new additions are quickly sold out by specialist growers. Towards the end of this month the most forward plants will require staking.

May

This is perhaps the busiest month in the delphinium calendar. Cuttings will be rooting and requiring potting. The earliest rooted plants will need their growing point removed. Seedlings should also be potted. Planting out the young plants of either seedlings or rooted cuttings should continue when the roots have filled the pots. Staking should now be completed, but remember to keep the uppermost ties on the loose side so that the spikes can sway in the wind.

May can be a very dry month. If you have mulched the soil after heavy rain early in the month and you possess a moisture-holding soil, then all will probably be well. On the other hand, if you have any doubt at all it is wise to see that your plants do not suffer through lack of water. Adequate moisture is perhaps the most important factor in producing vigorous plants.

Keen exhibitors will now be giving plants an extra feed if they are at all doubtful about their potential. A feed with a fairly high nitrogen content is often used to push up vegetative growth, balanced by a higher potash feed later in the month to assist in hardening the stems.

Do not forget to pay a visit to the Chelsea Flower Show, if you can make the journey, not only will you be able to see and order first class delphiniums, it is at this show that new introductions are first seen. A visit to the Delphinium Society's stand could also be worthwhile if you have any problems requiring an expert answer.

June

Continue to pinch out the growing point of rooted cuttings as they begin to run-up. Plant out young plants of named cultivars and seedlings. If space is at a premium, pot the plants into larger size pots, finishing with at least a 7 in. (18 cm), but preferably a 9 in. (23 cm) pot. Keep the hoe going and water all plants in periods of low rainfall, for they will now be growing at a tremendous rate. It is not at all uncommon for a developing spike to lengthen by as much as 3 in. (7.5 cm) a day. In favoured localities, especially in the south, the early cultivars will be showing colour by the middle of the month and, as a rough guide to assist the exhibitor, the spikes will be at their best seven to ten days from the time when the first floret matures. Autumn-sown seedlings will now begin to show their potential for many will be starting to elongate their spikes and the most forward ones may even begin to show colour towards the end of the month.

Try and spare the time to visit a specialist nurseryman or the garden of a delphinium enthusiast to compare notes and to see newer cultivars. Much can be learned about the delphinium by visiting any of the larger shows, especially those held in London by the Delphinium Society. Specimens of all types will be there for you to see, ranging from the shortest to the tallest, as well as classes restricting the colour of those spikes entered. The right question to experts on the stand could well save you not only time but a great deal of expense, for these amateur specialists are dedicated to the flower and their knowledge on all aspects is second to none. A trip to the Royal Horticultural Society's gardens at Wisley to see perhaps the most representative display is a delight, and glimpsing quantities of delphiniums in full bloom for the first time is an unforgettable experience.

July

Most of the remarks made for the previous month still apply, for June and July are the main flowering period. Late cultivars will be at their best towards the middle of this month. Study your autumn-sown seedlings carefully as they come into flower. Remove those which are obviously not up to standard immediately after flowering and make notes of those which you intend to leave in order that they can still be identified in the absence of their actual flower spike. If you fancy trying your hand at cross-pollination, the beginning of July is a good time, for laterals will still be available to work on from the earliest blooming plants, whereas late spikes will provide bottom florets to transfer pollen either to or from the plants of your chosen cross. As flowers begin to fade and are past their best, remove the main spike at a point just below the bottom faded floret. This will prolong the display of laterals and at the same time enhance their beauty. If selfed seed is required leave just one or two pods to develop as this will provide you with plenty; to allow all the florets to set seed naturally places an unnecessary strain on the plant.

Mildew may show on some cultivars and in some districts. If you find any of your plants are prone to this disease, which is unsightly if not serious, spray with a modern systemic fungicide. These newer chemicals are so effective that one application of spray is usually sufficient to control this disease.

As soon as the main display is over, and if you have been nursing new plants in large pots, lose no time in removing the old plants. Prepare the ground according to your inclination, bearing in mind the better you do this the better the foundation for the years ahead. It is essential to consolidate the soil well by treading before planting out the new bed. The newly planted delphiniums will almost certainly require a thorough watering to get them settled and growing away. A worthwhile experiment which can be very rewarding is to cut those plants which you intend to scrap for one reason or another at the end of the year down to ground level immediately after flowering. Give a generous application of a quick acting high nitrogen based fertilizer and thoroughly water the plants. New growth will appear at express speed and you will be rewarded with a second crop of flowers almost equal to the main display. Seasonal differences can, of course, play an important part in the flowering period, but plants treated in this manner will generally bloom in September. These delphiniums will survive and bloom again the following year at the normal time, but such drastic treatment will considerably reduce the quality and this experiment is only suggested if the plants are to be scrapped.

If you missed the opportunity to take orthodox cuttings in the early spring you can now propagate by eye cuttings. Approximately two weeks after cutting the flowered stems down to ground level lift the crown and secure the eyes or mini-minors as described in Chapter 4.

August

Tidy up and remove the part of the delphinium which has borne flowers. Watering is still very important in periods of drought to ensure that the crowns build up for next year's flowering.

Examine plants carefully for seed which is ripening. It may be necessary to protect the capsules from birds by means of a small bag or a piece of nylon stocking. Remove the pods as soon as they have turned light brown and finish the ripening process under cover. The seed may be sown late in the month when it has turned deep brown or blackish. Take care to keep sown seed in a cool place and aim at a temperature not much in excess of 60°F (15°C). Any surplus seed should be kept in a regrigerator where it will retain its viability until required.

September

Seed may still be sown and, after germinating, it can be brought into the warmer conditions of a greenhouse so that further progress can be made until the shorter hours of daylight stop the process altogether. Actual planting should only be done in the autumn in very light soils, unless the plants are from large plots. Small plants are best left in their pots until the spring. Seed sown in early spring will now be giving the raiser the greatest thrill, for the plants will start flowering this month if well grown. Take care with selection.

Slugs can start to be a nuisance with the damper conditions generally prevailing at this time of year. Constant warfare needs to be conducted from now on. If badly neglected, a solution of aluminium sulphate at the rate of 2 oz (55 g) per gallon should be watered on and around all frames and crowns in the open garden. Follow this up with a sprinkling of pellets based on methiocarb.

All seedlings and cuttings not planted out by September can usefully be housed in a frame with the lights sufficiently open to prevent heavy rain from puddling the soil in pots or seed trays. But the protection of a frame is not essential for the delphinium, however small, is perfectly hardy.

October

Spring-sown seed will still be giving a splendid display. Stakes used around mature delphiniums can now be removed and towards the end of the month a start can be made in cutting plants down to ground level and generally tidying up the delphinium borders. Continue to take action against slugs with methiocarb-based pellets.

November

Finally clean all delphinium borders and remove debris which acts as a hiding place for slugs. Continue to place small amounts of slug pellets around crowns. If really badly infested with slugs—frequently by a sign of neglect, for modern measures of control can eliminate this pest—remove the soil from around the crown and replace this with sharp grit. This protection is effective, for slugs will not cross such an abrasive surface. As with most other crops this month is a good time to prepare the soil for planting delphiniums next year. Only if drainage is suspect is it necessary to dig deeply; on light soils this can be harmful.

December

Nothing much to do this month unless the tidying-up process recommended earlier has been neglected. How about sitting back and enjoying those colour transparencies of your favourite plants or that wonderful seedling that is going to bring you fame and fortune (well, perhaps!) and that you are going to name after your spouse? Certainly a good month for reflection and for enjoying armchair delphinium-gardening. Make the most of it for in eight weeks, or even less, the whole wonderful cycle begins again.

12 The Delphinium Society and its Association with the Royal Horticultural Society

It is perhaps unusual in a book of this nature to devote a chapter to a Society formed exclusively to cater for enthusiasts of a particular flower. Yet the present-day economics of plant breeding and research mean that an organization like the Delphinium Society has an increasingly vital role to play. Gone are the days when a nursery could afford to subsidize research, raise new cultivars and generally promote a particular flower. Yet this work was commonplace between the wars and even continued for a short period after 1945. In the 1930s there were a large number of nurserymen specializing in the delphinium; now just one major specialist nursery exists, Blackmore & Langdon, and even in this case the future looks bleak so far as the delphinium is concerned. We saw earlier, too, how these same economic forces and the changing pattern of priorities may put in jeopardy the quest for the red hardy perennial garden delphinium. Happily, the Delphinium Society has no intention of letting these forces operate to the detriment of the flower and, as the professional fades from the delphinium scene, so the amateur, with increased leisure time at his disposal, will take over the role.

The Delphinium Society was formed in the autumn of 1928, ironically enough by a group of famous nurserymen. The aims of the Society have changed very little from the original objects which were 'to encourage the production of new and improved varieties; to collect and disseminate information; to organize and hold exhibitions; to keep a register of recognized named varieties; and to publish an annual journal'. Their first show was held in the Royal Horticultural Society's New Hall in 1929 and no fewer than thirteen nurseries staged exhibits. At that time there were also forty-four professional growers specializing in the flower who were active members. It was really a Society run by the trade and it was that section of the membership who not only influenced all decisions but who also stood to gain much from a thriving organization.

This domination of the delphinium by commerce continued throughout the 1930s, almost up to 1939, but since then dramatic changes have taken place: not only have the roles been reversed, but the amateur has completely taken over, except for the one specialist trade grower already mentioned. The most significant result of this change concerns the raising of new cultivars. Until recently, the bulk of new plants on trial at the Royal Horticultural Society's gardens at Wisley were raised by commercial sources; amateurs submitted a comparatively trivial number. The position today is quite different: it is the amateur who is raising the new and better cultivars, and the prospects are that new plants in the future will come entirely from non-trade sources.

The Wisley Trials

The delphinium has always played a significat part in the various trials of flowers at Wisley, which are run and maintained by the Royal Horticultural Society. A committee is elected each year consisting of a Chairman, a Vice-Chairman, six members representing the Royal Horticultural Society and eight officials of the Delphinium Society. In addition there is a Trials Officer who is responsible for the well-being of some 250 plants which are under his care. These trials never fail to impress the visitor and are an important 'shop window' for the critical examination of new cultivars.

It is not easy to have plants accepted for trial. Initially, under the present rules, a stipulated number of spikes have to be presented to the Joint Committee of the two societies in London on one of two specified days. This pre-judging is carried out to ensure that only very promising material is seen at Wisley. There are three categories:

a. As a show flower.
b. As a cultivar suitable for a cut flower.
c. As a cultivar suitable for ordinary garden purposes.

A delphinium can be entered under more than one of these headings. A successful raiser may be awarded a preliminary commendation in the case of a show flower, but in the other two categories an award will only be made after trial at Wisley.

The raiser then has to supply three young plants to the Trials Officer at Wisley, which are planted together with all the other delphiniums selected by the Joint Committee. Treatment of each plant is identical: fresh ground, superbly prepared, is used each year so that objective comparisons can be made. The year following planting is the one in which the raiser is likely to learn the fate of his plants. The trials are inspected by the Joint Committee on at least two occasions and each cultivar or named seedling is critically examined by experts. If the plants have performed well then the raiser may be fortunate enough to receive an award. These awards are, of course, coveted and are not given lightly. It may be that the Committee express some doubts, in which case he might well be asked to re-submit a further three plants the following year. It is also possible that the seedling may be considered inferior for one reason or another and it could be rejected and withdrawn from the trial.

But what if the plant is a real winner and the raiser does receive an award? Well, these are the categories. The premier award for a plant which is regarded as outstanding and is usually a decided break in a new direction is the First Class Certificate (F.C.C.). Next in descending order, is the Award of Merit (A.M.) and finally the Highly Commended (H.C.). It is extremely unlikely that a newly submitted plant will gain an F.C.C. in its first year. The more normal course even for an outstanding plant is a gradual moving up in assessment over a period of years.

The case of the cultivar 'Hilda Lucas' is extraordinary. This plant gained an A.M. in 1964 but, because it is perhaps the latest of all delphiniums to bloom, it was always in tight bud stage at the time of the visits of the Judging Committee—until 1978, that is, when a special visit was made to look at this superb cultivar. A unanimous vote was given to award it an F.C.C.—so a period of no less than fourteen years had elapsed before the plant gained the highest accolade—a testimony to the longevity of a tremendous plant and an insight into the cautious manner in which awards are given.

A further feature of the trials and of great significance is the register and the official description of the plants gaining awards. As a typical example let me refer again to 'Hilda Lucas'. It is registered as a tall cultivar and is described as follows:

'Hilda Lucas'. (Raised and introduced by the late Mr H.R. Lucas; sent by Messrs Ashton Nurseries.) F.C.C. 10th July, 1978. Plant 198.1 to 228.6 cm (6½ to 7½ ft) tall; flower spike 91.5 cm (3 ft) long, tapering, flowers closely spaced, many sidespikes; flowers 7.6 cm (3 in.) diameter, semi-double, on a very long stalk; outer sepals a colour slightly deeper than Blue Group 101C, flushed towards base with Violet Group 84C, inner sepals slightly deeper blue than Blue Group 100C heavily flushed and streaked with Violet Group 84C, some tips edged with black. Eye slightly deeper blue than Blue Group 100C, streaked with Violet Group 84C, some margins streaked with black. Flowering from 8th July, 1978 (A.M. 1964.)(60).

It is not generally appreciated, even by horticultural tradesmen, that the Royal Horticultural Society is the international body authorized solely by the International Horticultural Congress to maintain a register of delphiniums. This is usually strictly adhered to by all reputable raisers of delphiniums throughout the world. Indeed, those delphiniums which are not registered can nearly always be regarded with justifiable scepticism.

The Delphinium Society owes much to the Royal Horticultural Society and the cooperation between the two has always been a most happy and pleasant one.

13 List of Delphinium Species

The following descriptive table lists all the species of delphinium for which definite information is available. It is as accurate as time and research have permitted, for the greatest of care has been exercised over a period of many years, including direct reference to botanists from all parts of the world.

The question of synonyms is exceedingly complex. Where alternative spellings have been shown in brackets it may be assumed that these are quite reliable. There are, however, some species which will be found under different names and it would be unwise to be dogmatic in these cases.

For the sake of regularity it has been thought prudent to compile a second list of other recorded species where full details are either absent or the information may be questioned as to its authenticity. This appears on pages 174-5.

There are clearly many more species of delphinium scattered throughout the world, possibly hundreds, and it is my fervent hope, as well as that of John Neave, to whom I have extended by grateful thanks in the Acknowledgments, that these two lists will provide a unique starting point for the further research required.

Name	Description	Origin
DELPHINIUM **abietorum**		USA
aconitioides		Asia
aconitum *(D. aconitim)*	Purple and blue florets. 12 in. (30 cm)	Levant (1801)
acuminatissimum		Asia
aemulans		Asia, Afghanistan
ajacis *(D. aiacis, D. ajax)*	Mostly blue, but some pink varieties and many other shades and tints. 3 ft (90 cm)	Swiss Alps (1573)
–'Flore pleno'	Double flowered annuals in a wide range of colours.	
–'Hyacinthi- florum'	Of vigorous dwarf habit.	
–'Major'	The Rocket Larkspur.	
–'Minus'	Dwarf Rocket Larkspur.	
–'Roseum'	Double deep rose pink.	

Name	Description	Origin
DELPHINIUM **aitchisonii**	Named after Dr Aitchison who discovered *D. zalil* in Afghanistan in 1886.	Kashmir (1895)
albiflorum	White flowered. 4ft (120 cm)	America (1823)
albomarginatum	Dark violet-blue.	Tashkent
album	Cream and greenish-white. 15-30 in. (38-76 cm)	Turkish Armenia
alopecuroides	Bronzy-blue.	
alpestre	Florets mid-blue with yellow eye borne on stiff spikes above hairy foliage. 8 in. (20 cm)	Colorado (Mountains)
alpinum	Blue florets 5 ft (150 cm)	Hungary (1816)
altaicum	Blue florets.	Altai Mountains (1829)

Delphiniums

Name	Description	Origin
DELPHINIUM **altissimum**	Trusses of blue to purple florets borne on slender hairy branches. The plants grow on the highest mountain slopes—hence the name. 3 ft (90 cm)	Himalayas
–drepanocentrum		
–nipalensis *(D. altissimum nepalensis)*		
–phallutensis		
–walichie		
amabile	Light blue florets, similar to *D. scaposum*, which has dark blue florets.	
amanl		Syria (1894)
ambiguum *(D. ambigua)*	Blue flowers.	Barbary Coast (1759)

Name	Description	Origin
DELPHINIUM		
amoenum	Medium sized blue conical florets with straight spurs. 2 ft (60 cm)	Siberia (1818)
andersonii	Blue and purple florets on very stout stems. 3 ft (90 cm)	Columbia, America
antheroideum *(D. anthoroideum)*	Pale blue or mauve plus creamy-white	Kurdistan
anthora *(D. anthorgi)*		Europe and the Orient (H. Baillon, 1883)
anthriscifolium		China (1868)
apetalum		Turkestan (1895)
aruense	Florets white and blue.	
astaphisagria *(D. staphisagria, D. staphisagrie, D. scaphysagrye, D. stavesacre)*	Reddish-purple florets borne on long pedicels. A very poisonous plant yielding an alkaloid extract called delphine. Biennial or annual.	Southern Europe

Delphiniums

Name	Description	Origin
DELPHINIUM **atropurpureum**	(see *D. cashmirianum.*)	
aurantiacum	A variety of *D. nudicaule* (q.v.).	
azureum	Large light blue florets. 2-3 ft (60-90 cm)	Rocky Mountains, North America (1805)
–'Album'	A white form of the above.	
balansae		Algeria (1856) (Morocco to Tunis)
barbatum	Blue florets tinged green or white on stout stems.	Tashkent
–caeruleum		
–pallidum		
barbeyi	Florets purple and blue, also pink and white varieties.	Utah
barlowii	Raised by Mr Barlow of Manchester	
batalinii		Turkestan (Huth, 1895)

122

Name	Description	Origin
DELPHINIUM		
beesianum	Similar to *D. likiangense*. Dark purple-blue covered externally with grey hair.	Yunnan
belladonna	Origin unknown, but first mentioned in 1857 and offered by Kelways Nursery in 1880. A dainty plant with many thin wiry stems bearing the purest of blue florets. In 1900 a natural mutation occurred at the Royal Moerheim Nurseries, The Netherlands, and was cultivated by Mr Ruys, while the present race of Belladonnas originated in 1903 when Mr Gibson of Leeming Bar managed to secure three fertile seedpods from an inflorescence where chromosome doubling had accidentally happened. 4 ft (120 cm)	

Name	Description	Origin
DELPHINIUM **bellamosum**	Gentian-blue florets borne on loose spikes. Grows best in well-drained light soil. 3-4 ft (90-120 cm)	
bicolor	Upper petals cream veined blue; lower petals rich blue. Loose spikes. 12 in. (30 cm)	Wyoming to Alaska
biternatum **–leiocarpum**	Larger, but paler yellow florets than *D. zalil*.	Turkestan
blockmanae	Large white eyes in dense racemes.	California (1893)
bonvalotti		China (Franchet, 1893)
borbasii		Macedonia
brachycentron	Trusses of large blue flat florets. 2 ft (60 cm)	Siberia

Name	Description	Origin
DELPHINIUM		
brunoniamum	Hooded purple/violet or mauve florets, having hairy blue flecked eyes. Grows at 16,000 ft in Himalayas. Musky odour. 12 in. (30 cm)	Afghan Mountains, Tibet, Nepal (1864)
bucharicum	Pale bluish-white florets with very hairy lower petals.	Bishkent
bulleyanum	Rich blue-purple pubescent florets.	Yunnan, Szeechwan and mountain slopes in Northern Asia.
burkii	Discovered by Farrer growing near riversides. Indigo florets (synonymous with *D. diversicolor,* which is smaller, and *D. scopulorum).* 2 ft (60 cm)	California

Delphiniums

Name	Description	Origin
DELPHINIUM **calcicola**	Similar to *D. muscosum.* Hairy appearance of finely divided foliage.	Lichiang
californicum	White	
calleryi		China (Franchet, 1882)
camptocarpum *(D. camptocarpa)*	White or lilac pink.	Hindu Kush
candelabrum	Allied to *D. likiangense.* Sombre purple-brown florets.	Lichiang
candidum	(Synonymous *D. leroyi* cv. *D. candidum*) Powerful scent of *Narcissus* in habitat.	Abyssinia
cardinale	Wide open scarlet florets. 6-8 ft (180-240 cm)	California (1885) and west coast of America

Name	Description	Origin
DELPHINIUM (**cardinale** contd)		
–luteum	A yellow form of *D. cardinale* which was experimented with by Dr Melquist of California. He grew 20,000 plants over the period 1935-52 and still failed to produce a wholly satisfactory garden hybrid.	California (1885) and west coast of America
cardiopetalum	(Synonymous with *D. barteratum* and *D. verdunense*.) An annual bearing blue and purple florets with heartshaped petals. 12 in. (30 cm)	Mediter- ranean region (1818)
carolinium *(D. carolinianum*	(Synonymous with *D. penhardii* (the elusive white variety) and *D. azureum*.) Medium blue florets. 2 ft (60 cm)	North Carolina and southwards
carporum	Cylindrical spikes of white and pink florets over downy foliage. 12 in. (30 cm)	Western Rocky Mountains

Name	Description	Origin
DELPHINIUM		
cashmeriana *(D. cashmiriana, D. cashmirianum)*	Various colours such as deep blue, light blue, light and dark purple with dark eyes. A dwarf stoloniferous plant.	Kashmir and Himalayas (Royle, 1839)
cashmirianum *(D. atro-purpureum)*	Light blue single florets striped dark blue and having a yellow eye. Each stem bears only one flower. 12 in. (30 cm)	Himalayas (Lindner, 1929)
–royle		Kashmir
–walkeri		
catsienense	(See *D. tatsienense.*) Rich indigo florets and attractive bottle green foliage. 20 in. (50 cm)	Szechuan
caucasicum	Azure blue with purple outer petals and white eye. Each flower borne on a single stalk. 4 in. (10 cm)	Caucasus
–tanguticum		

viii The author's garden

ix Close-up of a University hybrid

x A University hybrid growing in
the 'open'

xi An arrangement of University
hybrids by Mrs Lilian Radley

xii Close-up of a University hybrid

xiii 'Cream Cracker'

xiv A pink seedling raised by
the author

xv 'Crown Jewel'

xvi 'Michael Ayres'

xvii 'Turkish Delight'

xviii 'Chelsea Star'

xix 'Hilda Lucas'

xx 'Silver Jubilee'

xxi 'Blue Nile'

xxii 'Mighty Atom'

xxiii 'Loch Leven'

xxiv 'Gillian Dallas'

xxv A pink seedling raised by the author

Name	Description	Origin
DELPHINIUM **certatophorum**	Lax racemes of dark blue florets spurs coiled in a loop.	Yunnan (1886)
chefoense		China (1893)
cheilanthum	Dark blue florets with pale yellow or white eye, branching habit. 3 ft (90 cm)	Siberia (1819)
chinensis *(D. chinense)*	(Synonymous with *D. grandiflorum,* q.v.)	
cinereum	Pale blue and pubescent florets.	Turkey
coccineum	(Synonymous with *D. cardinale*, q.v.)	San Diego (C.C. Parry, 1850)
cockerelii	Large metallic purple florets on a handsome bush with gummy foliage. 4 ft (120 cm)	Southern Colorado

Name	Description	Origin
DELPHINIUM		
coelestinum	Azure-blue florets and finely divided foliage. 4 ft (120 cm)	East Szechuan
coeruleum aconitum	Cambridge-blue florets on graceful branching spikes. 12 in. (30 cm)	Sikkim and Tibet
cognatum		America (1897)
columbianum	(Probably synonymous with *D. ajacis*)	
confertiflorum	Has a shorter denser column of smaller florets than *D. amabile*.	
confertifolium	(Probably synonymous with *D. ajacis*)	
consolida	The branching larkspur. White to purple originally, but now obtainable in many colours. Indigenous to northern Europe, it could almost qualify as a native of England!	

Name	Description	Origin

DELPHINIUM (consolida contd)

−coccineum — Rich rose scarlet blossoms.

−flore pleno — Double flowered variegated variety of above.

−eranthemus

−imperialis

−regalis

−flore pleno

−sylvestris

cordiopetalum — (See *D. cardiopetalum.*)

cossonianum — Dense racemes of white and violet. — Canary Islands, Algeria, Syria, Morocco

crassicaule — A thick stemmed plant with blue florets. — Siberia (1822)

cuneatum — Wedge-shaped leaves and blue florets. — Siberia (1822)

cyanoreios — Lighter and more brilliant blue than *D. simplex.*

131

Name	Description	Origin
DELPHINIUM cyphoplectrum	Pale blue to dark violet. 18-14 in. (45-100 cm)	Eastern Caspian area, S.W. Iran, S.E. Turkey
−micranthum		
−pallidiflorum		
−stenophyllum		
−tuberosum		
−vanense		
dasyanthum	Brilliant blue florets, short sparse downy foliage. 18 in. (45 cm).	Turkestan
−augustisectum		
−undulatum	Grows at 12,500 ft, colour subdued blue. 3 ft (90 cm)	Hindu Kush
dasycarpum	Similar to *D. elatum*; soft blue with dark brown eye. 4-6 ft (120-180 cm)	Caucasus (1819)

Name	Description	Origin
DELPHINIUM **dasycaulon**	Small blue with short spurs. Grows in grass-lands and wooded clearings.	Africa: Ethiopia and southwards, Tanganyika, Kenya and Sudan
dasystachyum	Florets deep indigo, cobalt-blue and pale greeny-blue. 12 in. (30 cm)	Kop-Dagh
−longebracteatum		
−ochroleucum	Yellowy-white variety.	Turkestan and Caucasus
−szovitzianum		
davidii	Deep blue florets, ranunculus leaved foliage.	Eastern Tibet
davisii	Blue to violet. Discovered by Dr Mung and named in honour of P.H. Davis.	Turkey
decorum	Deep blue or violet with yellow eye. A Slender, graceful plant. 18 in. (45 cm)	Russia (1838), also California

Delphiniums

Name	Description	Origin

DELPHINIUM (decorum contd)
–deparperatum

–menziesii

–patens

delawayi	Hirsute (hairy) plant bearing bright blue florets. 12 in. (30 cm)	Yunnan

–acuminatum

–aureum

denudatum	Branching, yellow sepals, blue petals.	Himalayas
depauperatum		California
desertii	yellow flowers.	Sinai Peninsula

–syriaca

*devaricatum		Caspian, Iran and Caucasus (1836)

* Probably synonymous with *divaricatum* (see p. 135)

134

Name	Description	Origin

DELPHINIUM (**devaricatum** contd)

–cinereum

–glandulesum

–laxiflorum

–proprium

–tibeticum

–uralense

divaricatum	Sparse small florets of deep violet-blue and purple-blue on slender branching stems. An annual	

–canescens

–glaberrimum

–pubiflorum

dictyocarpum *(D. dyctyscarpum*	Pale blue florets on supple leafy stems. 2 ft (60 cm)	Caucasus and Siberia (de Candolle, 1817)
discolor	Blue and white (bi-coloured). 6 ft (180 cm)	Siberia (1834)

Name	Description	Origin
DELPHINIUM **distichum**	Pale blue florets on tall erect plant; found in damp and boggy meadows at foot of mountain ranges.	Rocky Mountains
diversicolor	Plant with a sticky, leafy stem. Similar but smaller florets than *D. burkii*. 18 in. (45 cm)	
duhmbergii **–retropilosum**	Racemes of white or blue florets over a long period (June-August). 2-6 ft (60-180 cm)	Russia and Turkestan
elatius	Variety of *D. nudicaule*.	
elatum	Grows on stony mountain slopes. European distribution from Pyrenees to Siberia. Florets a delightful cornflower blue with yellow bearded eyes peeping from the small but wide open florets. 6 ft (180 cm)	Swiss Alps (1597)

Name	Description	Origin
DELPHINIUM (elatum contd)		
−elegans	Blue florets 18 in. (45 cm)	North America (1741)
−flore pleno	Similar, but with double florets.	
−emiliae	Similar to *D. grandiflorum* in habit. Pale or dark blue. 12-18 in. (30-45 cm)	Western California (Redwood areas)
emarginatum	Bluish-lilac	Africa
eriostylum	Tall, robust perennial with blue florets.	Kweichow, China
exaltatum	Violet-blue florets on slim spikes. 12-36 in. (30-90 cm)	North America (1758)
−nuttallii	Yellow-eyed, deep blue florets on long sprays. 2 ft (61 cm)	Wooded banks of the Columbia River, North America
fargesii	The brilliant blue florets have hairy spurs and are arranged spirally on the well-packed spike. 12 in. (30 cm)	Szechuan

137

Name	Description	Origin
DELPHINIUM **fissum**	Blue florets on a slender spike. Probably a blue variety of *D. zalil*. Long flowering period (June–September). 3 ft (90 cm)	Hungary (1816), Eastern Transylvania
−anatolicum		
flavum *(D. flavis)*	Yellow florets.	Syria and Iran
flexuosum	Blue florets. 2 ft (61 cm)	Caucasus (1820)
flexuotum		Armenia
foliosum		California (1863)
formosum	Violet-blue florets. A graceful plant with handsome grey-green foliage.	Swiss Alps
forrestii	Pale water-blue florets. Similar to *D. densiflorum* and *D. pellucidum*. Florets also are large and hairy, leaves rounded.	

Name	Description	Origin
DELPHINIUM		
freynii	Bright blue florets. 12 in. (30 cm)	Caucasus
geraniifolium	Dark blue florets, late in flower. 12 in. (30 cm)	Rockies
geyeri	Azure florets with yellow eyes, spikes springing from woolly tufts. This is a very poisonous plant. 18 in. (45 cm)	
gipsophylum *(D. gypsophylum)*		California
glabratum	Large hairy deep azure-blue florets. 3 ft (90 cm)	Himalayas
glabreosum *(D. glabrosum, D. glareosum)*	Deep purple-blue florets. A native of the USA. 8 in (20 cm)	Northern California, Oregon

Name	Description	Origin
DELPHINIUM **glaciale**	Bears a few large hairy florets of mid-blue on leafy stem. Has a scent of musk. 9 in. (23 cm)	Sikkim Alps and America
glandulosa *(D. glandulosum*	Purple florets.	Armenia
gorganicum *(D. gombaultii)*	Yellow florets.	Iran
gracile	Red florets.	Spain (1826)
gracilentum	Two or three fine florets per stem. 2-8 in. (5-20 cm)	Nevada, USA
grandiflorum	(Synonymous with *D. chinensis*, *D. chinense*, *D. sinense)*. Dark-blue, wide open florets. Several named cultivars available such as 'Blue Butterfly', 'Blue Gem' and the Cambridge blue 'Azure Fairy'. 2 ft (60 cm)	Russia, China, Siberia (1818)

Name	Description	Origin

DELPHINIUM (grandiflorum contd)

–album
An albino or white-flowered form.

–album pleno
Double white.

–cineraria
(D. coeruleum)
A beautiful Cambridge blue dwarf.
6-9 in. (15-25 cm)
M. Gaugin of Orleans introduced this plant in 1901 under the name of 'Blauer Spiegel' ('Blue Mirror'). It grows well on light sandy soil rich in humus.

–flore pleno
A double dark blue.
2 ft (60 cm)

–pallidum
Pale blue florets.

–rubrum
Red and pink florets.
3 ft (90 cm)

griseum
Whitish florets

halophila
(D. halophilum)
Pale mauve or cream florets. The name implies it is a lover of salt.
18 in. (45 cm)

Iranian
Kurdistan

Name	Description	Origin

DELPHINIUM

hamatum
Large pale blue florets with golden eyes and very curly spurs. The plant bears its beautiful flowers on slender stems and grows among limestone rocks.
6 in. (15 cm)

Origin: Yunnan

hansenii
Similar to *D. hesperium.* Pinky-mauve florets with blue-tipped sepals, borne in clusters on slender stems.

Origin: California

hebecarpum
(D. aquilegifolium)

Origin: Europe and Orient (1883)

henryi
Bears one or two large *D. grandiflorum* type florets on a slender leafy 9 in. (23 cm) stem. Likes a shady spot.

hesperium
Similar to *D. hansenii.* Lovely clear blue florets and also a white form.
2 ft (60 cm)

Origin: Southern California

–recurvatum
A pink-flowered type

Origin: Southern California

Name	Description	Origin

DELPHINIUM
hillcoatiae

A species named by Dr Munz in honour of Miss Hillcoat who had given him so much help when studying the delphinium species recorded in the Botany Department of the British Museum.
The plant had been dis-covered by Ludlow and Sherriff in 1936 grow-ing at a height of 11,000 ft on a dry stony hillside at Kap, Chayul Chu in Southern Tibet. This same plant had also been found on slate screes in the Nye Chu valley, Chayul Dzong (Tibet) by the famous plant hunter Kingdon-Ward in 1935. The simple spire bore glandular sepals of white tinged green and each sepal had a bright green tip; the spurs are pale green in colour.
In flower late July and again in September.

Tibet (1935)

Name	Description	Origin
DELPHINIUM hirschfeldianum		Aegina (Szyszyl- owicz, 1888)
hirsutum	A hairy plant.	
hispanicum parvum	Foliage like the Scabious.	
hohenackeri		Asia Minor (1867)
holopetalum		Macedonia (Boissier, 1841)
hui	Greenish-purple sepals, dull yellow upper petals.	Peiping
hybridum	Blue florets bearded below with white, white eye. Very long straight spurs and a bulbous root. Similar to *D. cheilanthum* and *D. elatum.*	Mountain ranges of Asia, Turkestan and Siberia (1794)

Name	Description	Origin

DELPHINIUM (hybridum contd)

−ochroleucum (Synonymous with *D. albiflorum.*) Creamy white. — Armenia

iliense
  (D. ibiense) — Turkestan (1895)

−augustatum

−hispidum

−macrocentrum

−pubiflorum

incana
  (D. incanum) — India

intermedium (Synonymous with *D. elatum.*) Blue. — Silesia (1794)

−caerulescens Light blue florets and downy foliage. 7 ft (210 cm) — (1836)

−laxum Loose spikes bearing blue forets. 6 ft (180 cm)

−ranunculifolium

ithaburnense — Syria (1849)

Name	Description	Origin
DELPHINIUM kingianum		India (Bruhl, 1894)
knorringianum	Tall and slender, florets less brilliant than those of *D. grandiflorum*	
labrangense	Alpine plants forming foot-high mounds of blue to purple florets.	Yunnan
lanigerum		Iran
latisepaum	Compact inflorescence of large deep blue florets.	Mexico
laxiflorum	Similar to *D. dictyo-carpum,* but has larger pale blue florets. The plant has thick leathery leaves.	Altai Mountains and Siberia
leiocarpum		Siberia (1893)
leonardii	A *D. menzesii* type.	Idaho

Name	Description	Origin
DELPHINIUM **leptophyllum**	Deep blue florets on very long pedicels. The florets seem to float in the air like butterflies.	Mexican Highlands
leptostachyum	Blue florets. 6 ft (180 cm)	Pyrenees
–pallidum	Pale blue. 2 ft (60 cm).	
–pilosissimum	Hirsute (hairy) plant with blue florets. 6 ft (180 cm)	Siberia
–ranunculifolium	Leaf structure similar to buttercup. Blue florets.	Pyrenees
–sapphirinum	Sapphire-blue florets. 7 ft (210 cm)	
leroyi	Sweetly perfumed pale blue florets on branching stems. (Synonymous *D. candidum* applies to the scented white variety.)	Kenya and Uganda

Delphiniums

Name	Description	Origin
DELPHINIUM **likiangense**	Three to five large clear gentian blue florets on short racemes borne on stiff spikes above finely cut foliage. Strongly scented of hyacinth. Grows among rocks at height of 5000-6000 ft. (Similar to *D. beesianum, D. calcicola, D. candelabrum* and *D. labrangense.*) 12-15 in. (30-38 cm)	Yunnan and Lichiang, Northern China
longipedun- culatum		Turkestan (1877)
longipes		China (1886)
loscosii		Spanish Alps (1873)
luporum	(Synonymous *D. scopulorum.*)	
luteum	(Synonymous *D. nudicaule luteum.*) Pale yellow florets.	California

Name	Description	Origin
DELPHINIUM **mackianum**	A violet form of *D. elatum.*	Siberia
macrocentron *(D. macro-centrum)*	Droopy large florets in a strange variety of colours. Colours noted so far are bluey-green, yellowy-green, electric-blue, sea-green, peacock-blue and turquoise. 6 ft (180 cm)	East Africa
macrostachyum	The bronzy-black florets are held aloft. A white tassle of styles is set off by black anthers bearing a profuse quantity of creamy pollen. 4 ft (120 cm)	Iraq, Iranian Kurdistan
maydellianum		Siberia (1879)

Name	Description	Origin
DELPHINIUM menzesii *(D. menziesii)*	Similar to *D. decorum.* Large mid-blue florets on slender stems. The plant has a fleshy root and the seeds can take as long as a year to germinate. 12 in. (30 cm)	California and West Coast of America to British Columbia (1826)
mesoleucum	Blue florets with white eyes. 3 ft (90 cm)	(1822)
middendorfii	The blue florets have long sepals and the eyes are striped yellow and blue. 2-3 ft (60-90 cm)	Siberia
midzonense		Europe (1898)
monogynum	(Synonymous *D. aconitum.*)	
montanum	(Synonymous *D. elatum.*) Blue florets. 4 ft (120 cm)	Switzerland (1819)

Name	Description	Origin
DELPHINIUM (montanum contd)		
–bracteosum	Blue florets. 3 ft (90 cm).	Southern Europe (1816)
moschatum	Dark blue florets. Musky scent. 6 ft (180 cm)	Switzerland (1834)
mosoynense		China (1893)
muscosum	Solitary florets on about twenty stems. Foliage lace and mossy appearance.	Bhutan (Sherriff, 1949)
nanum	Long spurred blue-flowered annual. An Egyptian species, grows in quite arid areas.	Western Mediter-ranean
narbonense		Swiss Alps (1893)
nelsonii	Hairy blue florets on slender stems. Similar in habit to *D. menzesii* and *D. glabreosum.*	North America: Nebraska

Name	Description	Origin

DELPHINIUM

nortonii — A cluster of stems bearing large puffed-out solitary florets of violet. Grows up to 16,000 ft in Sikkim Alps. 4 in. (10 cm) — Sikkim

nudicaule — Half-closed vermilion-scarlet florets with yellow eye. 18 in. (45 cm) — Oregon, San Francisco, California

–aurantiacum

–'Chamois' — Apricot.

–elatius — A variety superior in brilliance and stature. (1870)

–luteum — Clear lemon-yellow. This species was described by Torrey and Gray in 1838 and introduced to horticulturists in 1870. Mr Ruys of Moerheim, Holland crossed this species with *D. elatum* and produced the hybrid known as 'Pink Sensation'. 3 ft (90 cm)

Name	Description	Origin

DELPHINIUM (nudicaule contd)

–**'Orange Queen'** Vivid pure orange.

nuristanicum *(D. nuristanica)*	Racemes of large brilliant blue, dark centres. Thin seeds with yellow wings. 2 ft (60 cm)	Afghanistan
obcordatum	Deep violet-blue florets. Grows in sandy, rocky areas of North African Coast.	Morocco, Algeria, Spain
occidentale	Closely set blue florets. 18 in. (45 cm)	China
ochroleucum	Lemon-yellow florets. 2 ft (60 cm)	Caucasus, Iberia, Georgia, Turkestan, Siberia, China (1823)
oliganthum *(D. oligantha)*		Syria (1867)
oliverianum *(D. oliveriana)*	Blue florets. 18 in. (45 cm)	Southern Europe (1826)

Name	Description	Origin
DELPHINIUM **oneophilum** *(D. oreophilum)*		Bokhara (1895)
oranense	Blue to violet florets. A variety of *D. cardio-petalum.*	Oran, Algeria
orientale *(D. orientalis)*	Brilliant though small, rich purple florets, borne on slender branching stems above the finely divided foliage. Its natural background of white limestone hills would accentuate the glowing purple florets of this elegant plant. (Dried specimen found in tomb of King Ahmes I still retained its colour from 1700 BC !!.) 3 ft (90 cm)	Turkeŝtan
ornatum	Prolific seed production in single pods.	

Name	Description	Origin
DELPHINIUM		
orthocentron	Branching stems bear long spurred pale blue florets. (Similar in habit to *D. tatsienense*, q.v.) 18 in. (45 cm)	Sutchuen
oxypetalum	Pale blue florets with black eye. Hairy appearance. 9-12 in. (23-30 cm)	Central Europe
oxysepalum	Probably synonymous with above.	Hungary (1891)
pallidum	Pale blue.	Siberia (1822)
palmatifidium	Leaves shaped like human hands. 3-4 ft (90-120 cm)	Siberia (1824)
–glabellum	Smooth foliage and blue florets. 3-4 ft (90-120 cm)	Siberia (1817)
paludicola	Smaller and less striking than *D. tibeticum* (q.v.)	Himalayas

Name	Description	Origin
DELPHINIUM **paniculatum**		Iran, Macedonia
paphlagonicum		China
paradoxum		Turkestan (Bunge, 1851)
pardonii	The blue florets are well spaced on the racemes.	China
parishii	Large brilliant blue florets on narrow spikes. Sparsely foliaged. 18 in. (45 cm)	California
parryi	Large deep blue florets on graceful stems. 2 ft (60 cm)	California
pauciflorum	Bright blue florets with yellow eyes, borne on slender stems. 12 in. (30 cm)	Colorado
pauperculum	Few florets on fragile, slender stems. Grows at Alpine levels in the Oregon Mountains.	Oregon

Name	Description	Origin
DELPHINIUM **penhardii**	A white variety of *D. carolinium*. Reputed to be an elusive plant to find in habitat.	Colorado, Texas, Arizona, Western America
pentagynum	Blue florets with five styles. 2 ft (60 cm)	Southern Europe (1819)
peregrinum	Blue florets. 12 in. (30 cm)	Italy (1629), Malta, Sicily
–bovei		
–eriocarpum		
–foskolii		
–subvelutinum		
–sunceum		
persicum *(D. persica)*	Rosy-mauve florets.	Elburz Mountains

Name	Description	Origin
DELPHINIUM **pictum**	(see *D. requieni.*)	
poltaratskii		Turkestan (1869)
polyanthum	Blue florets with yellow bearded eyes.	Yunnan (1962)
przewaldskii	Pale yellow florets tipped with blue. 12-24 in. (30-60 cm)	Mongolia
pseudo- **peregrinum**	Red florets. 3 ft (90 cm).	Siberia (1823)
pseudotongalense	Yellowy-blue and blue florets.	Yunnan (1962)
pubescens	Blue florets on a downy plant.	Mediter- ranean (1816)
pubiflorum	Pale blue, rose or lilac florets.	Tunisia and Southern Europe
−dissitiflorum		
punicei	A yellow variety of *D. puniceum.*	Black Sea and Caspian Sea

Name	Description	Origin

DELPHINIUM (punicei contd)
– ochroleucis

puniceum — The purplish-red florets on this plant almost give it a black appearance. 12 in. (30 cm) — Siberia (1785), Georgia to Volga River

purpusii — Purple or muddy pink florets (diploid). This is possibly a *D. nudicaule hybrid.* — California (1895)

pycnocentrum — Blue florets on a tall, slender plant. Less brilliant than *D. grandiflorum.* —

pylzowii — Masses of violet-blue florets, hairy stems. (Similar to *D. likiangense.*) 9-12 in. (23-30 cm) — Kansu Province (China)

pyramidatum — — Caucasia (1891)

quercetorum — — Kurdistan (Boissier, 1888)

Name	Description	Origin
DELPHINIUM **ranunculae florum**	Double florets, bronzy-lilac and cobalt-blue.	
recurvatum	A pink variety of *D. hesperium* (diploid).	
requieni	Branching stems with bluey-white flowers. The florets have pink and green markings and are borne on 2-3 ft (60-90 cm) stems. Annual or biennial.	South-western Europe and Majorca (1824)
revolutum	Pale blue florets curled back. 6 ft (180 cm)	
rugulosum *(D. rugulosa)*	White flushed pink in loose racemes. Grows at heights of 5000 ft.	Afghanistan, Elburz Mountains
saniculifolium	Pale to dark blue florets on tall, narrow stems.	Hindu Kush Afghanistan
savatieri		China (1882)
savatile	Deep blue pubescent florets.	Szechwan

Name	Description	Origin

DELPHINIUM

scaposum

Floriferous racemes of dark blue florets on leafless stems. Grows in hot, dry places.
2 ft (60 cm)

schlagintocitii

Kashmir
(Huth, 1893)

Scopulorum

Similar in many respects to *D. elatum*. Grows on stony mountain slopes throughout Europe. (*D. burkii* is the white variety.) *D. scopulorum* also grows beside streams in the pasturelands of California and has indigo florets. Foliage is glaucous.
4 ft (120 cm)

California

−glaucum

−luporum

Name	Description	Origin
DELPHINIUM **semibarbatum**	This plant may be synonymous with or closely related to the following species: *D. sulphureum, D. zalil, D. ochroleucum, D. hoeltzeri* and *D. biternatum.*	
simplex	Blue florets with white eyes (similar to *D. scaposum*). Remarkable browny-black seeds with white wings. 2-3 ft (60-90 cm)	Idaho and Oregon Mountains
sinense	Deep blue double florets. (Dwarf form of *D. grandiflorum.*)	China
–flore pleno		
sinovitifolium	Blue florets on a slender hairy stem.	Szechwan
skaisiflorum		China (1876)
skirmantii		Algeria (1875)

Name	Description	Origin
DELPHINIUM **somcheticum**		Caucasia (1895)
sonnei		America (1897)
soulei	Spikes densely furnished with florets having the upper petals pale blue and the lower petals dark blue. (Not having seen the flowers growing it is not clear whether the 'petals' are the eye petals or perhaps the outer 'sepals'.) A most unusual miniature delphinium. The leaves are quite smooth, but the flower stem is hirsute. 6 in. (15 cm)	Dry areas of Szechwan
speciosum	4 in. (10 cm)	Caucasus
spirocentrum	Purplish-blue florets.	Yunnan, Szechwan
–grandibrac- teolatum		

Name	Description	Origin
DELPHINIUM (**spirocentrum** contd) **–hirsutum**		
–pediforme		
–pauciflorum		
spurium	Blue florets. 4 ft (120 cm)	Siberia (1810)
stapeliosum		Assam (Bruhl, 1894)
–khasianum		
–shanicum		
–siamense		
staphisagria	This poisonous annual is in a class of its own, in that it looks more like a lupin than a delphinium.	Eastern Mediterranean (1596)
stenosepalum		Kamchatka (1894)
stocksianum *(D. stocksiana)*	White florets. 15-24 in. (38-60 cm). Similar to *D. ajacis*, *D. amabile*, *D. confertiflorum*, and *D. xyllorhizum*.	River Oxus

Name	Description	Origin
DELPHINIUM		
suave	Large pale blue florets with creamy white flower petals and a white eye to each floret. A multitude of short 12 in. (30 cm) stems or spikes rise from the single crown.	Afghanistan
subglobosum	Scanty foliage. Transitional between *D. parishii* and *D. parryi* (q.v.)	
sulcatum		(Professor Reichenback, 1886)
sulphureum	Pale yellow florets. Similar to *D. ochroleucum* and *D. zalil.* 5 ft (150 cm)	Syria
sylvaticum	Loose racemes of lively blue florets.	Tunisia and Eastern Algeria
syncarpum		Iran (1886)

Name	Description	Origin
DELPHINIUM szovitzianum	Yellow hairy florets.	Armenia and Iran
taliense		China (1893)
tanguiticum	Rich violet-blue florets with white eyes. The plant produces a vast quantity of flower spikes and is somewhat similar in habit to *D. caucasicum*, being only 4 in. (10 cm) high.	Kansu and Szechuan
tatsienense *(D. tatsiense, D. tatsuenense, D. tatsuense)*	Long spurred florets of cornflower-blue (azure tips) borne on gracefully branched racemes. 12-18 in. (30-45 cm)	Szechuan
tauricum	Probably another blue variety of *D. hybridum*	Russia (1842)
tenuisectum		Mexico (E.L. Greene, 1894)

Name	Description	Origin
DELPHINIUM		
tenuissimum	Violet-blue florets on very slender stems and arranged in loose panicles.	Greece (Dr Sibthorpe, 1836)
thirkeanum	Mauve and white flowers.	Kurdistan
tibeticum	Slender stems bearing deep blue florets. Foliage thread-like. (Synonymous *D. mosoynense* and *D. paludicola.*) 2 ft (60 cm)	Tibet
tongolense		China (1893)
tribracteolatum		Mediterranean, Morocco and Algeria
tricorne	Florets of rich blue with white eye having blue veining. Flowers in the spring and then the whole plant ripens off and disappears into an underground tuber. This is a poisonous plant.	North America (Atlantic Coast) (1806)

Name	Description	Origin
DELPHINIUM **trigonelloides**		Iran (Boissier, 1841)
trilobatum		Himalayas (Huth, 1893)
triste	This grows in the mountainous regions bordering the Bering Sea. The florets are mahogany-red and edged with brown; the spurs are violet and the leaves a dark glossy green giving an overall effect of sombreness. The growth habit is extraordinary since the seeds germinate well and cotyledons appear then die away for a month. True leaves sprout up from the soil and they too die away. Later on larger leaves appear and the plant seems to have sufficient strength in the root system to support a flower spike. 12-24 in. (30-60 cm)	Siberia (1819)

Name	Description	Origin
DELPHINIUM		
trollifolium	Half-closed dark blue florets with white eye. Downy florets over foliage resembling that of the 'Trollius' plant. 12 in. (30 cm)	Columbia River, North America
tsarongense	Similar to *D. glaciale*, *D. chrysotrichum* and also *D. likiangense*, but the florets are much larger being perhaps the largest florets (over 2 in. (5 cm) diameter) of the delphinium species. The colour is water-blue veined with green and the florets have a hairy appearance. The flowers are scented in their habitat.	Armenia and Chinese Alps
turcmenum	Blue or bluey-white florets, sparse slender foliage. 12 in. (30 cm)	Near East
tyrolensis *(D. tiroliense)*	Blue florets on dwarf stems.	Austrian Tyrol

Name	Description	Origin
DELPHINIUM ucranicum	Blue florets.	Siberia (1818)
uechtritzianum		Serbia (1881)
uglinosum *(D. ulignosum' D. uliginosum)*	A dwarf species with blue florets. Broadly lobed foliage. Grows in damp gravelly water-courses 'in situ'.	Western America (1811)
urceolatum	Blue, pitcher-shaped florets. 2 ft (60 cm)	(1801)
vanensis		Kurdistan
variegatum *(D. variegata)*	Large purple florets, sometimes lavender or rosy-mauve. Flowers borne on a loose raceme, simple or branched. Known in America as the Royal Larkspur.	California
velutinum	Blue florets with a velvety texture. 4 ft (120 cm)	Italy (1819)

Name	Description	Origin
DELPHINIUM		
venenosum	Dark blue spikes in high summer. The stem rises from a small tuber. 2 ft (60 cm)	
venulosum	Blue florets.	Asia Minor, Anatolia and Turkey (1867)
verdunense	(Synonymous *D. halteratum.*)	
vestitum	Deep violet florets on a stately spike. Farrer says it has a white eye, Sampson Clay says it has a brown or dark eye. 4-5 ft (120-150 cm)	Himalayas, North India, Afghanistan, North China, Western America
–hirsutum		
–pumilum		
–sphenolobum		
villosum	Brownish-purple florets with yellow bearded eyes. The colour combination is unusual and striking.	Caucasus, Altai Mountains, Russia, Turkestan (1818)

171

Name	Description	Origin
DELPHINIUM		
vimineum	Similar to *D. carolinium.* Dazzling azure florets held on branching stems. 3 ft (90 cm)	Texas
virescens	Almost identical to the elusive *D. penhardii.*	Canada
−albescens		
viride		Mexico (S. Watson, 1888)
virgatum	Blue florets. 18 in. (45 cm)	Syria (1823)
viscidum	Branched heads or corymbs of dark blue rise above the sticky grey-haired foliage.	Plains of Wyoming
viscosum	A striking large Himalayan species; florets are cream or pale yellow with contrasting dark eyes.	Himalayas
−ciliata		

Name	Description	Origin

DELPHINIUM (viscosum contd)
−chrysatrichum

−connectens

−gigantabracteum

vitifolium   china

Name	Description	Origin
wardii	Medium size violet florets. The whole plant is hirsute (hairy). 9 in. (23 cm)	
welbeyi *(D. welbyi, D. wellbeyi, D. wellbyi)*	Bright blue florets toned mauve and light blue. Scented in habitat.	Abyssinia
yunnanens *(D. yunnanense)*	The florets are an intense blue with very long spurs and have light brown eyes. A straggly plant flowering until October. 24 in. (60 cm)	Yunnan, China and Tibet

Name	Description	Origin
zalil	The most beautiful yellow species introduced to the Western world. The florets are a pure sulphur yellow with orange tips to the central petals of each floret. 3-4 ft (90-120 cm)	Afghanistan and Iran (Dr Aitchinson, 1888)

Species of Delphinium where full details are not available

D. antheroides
aqueligifolium
armeniaca
axilliflorum
axilliflora
biternatum
bithynicum
bovei
brownii
burmanese
buschianum
ciliatum
chrysotrichum
coerulescens
conspicuum
cooperi
cornuta

D. corymbosum
densiflorum
dumetorum
dyctiocarpum
glaberrimum
englerianum
hoffmeisteri
incisum
simplex
eriocarpum
erlangshanicum
esquirolii
exiguum
exsertum
fangshanense
flavescens
gayanum

D. georgii
  halteratum
    venulosum
  verdunense
  ilganzense
  jacquemontianum
  jugorum
  junceum
  kamonense
  kantzeense
  karataviense
  karateginii
  kawaguchii
  keteleeri
  laxum
  leptocarpa
  leucosepalum
  lynarioides
  ochroleucum

D. ochrolinum
  ochrolinum sulphureum
  olopetala
  palmatum
  parygia
  pellucidum
  patens
  pusilla
  raveyi
  regalis
  schlagintweitii
  sclerioclada
  stenocarpasaccata
  sulphurea
  teheranica
  tomentosa
  vanense
  verdunense
  vulgae
  xyllorhizum

List of Addresses

The Delphinium Society
11 Long Grove
Seer Green
Beaconsfield
Bucks.

The undermentioned horticultural societies are affiliated to the Delphinium Society and usually display delphiniums in separate classes at their annual shows.

Ainsdale Horticultural Society
Miss C.E. Ainsworth
473 Liverpool Road
Birkdale
Southport
Lancs

Alderley Edge and Wilmslow Horticultural Society
Miss E.A. Donoghue
19 The Race
Handforth
Wilmslow
Cheshire

Arundel Gardens Association
'Greenwillow'
72 Ford Road
Arundel
Sussex

Banstead Horticultural Society
H.J. Green Esq
37 Waterer Gardens
Burgh Heath
Tadworth
Surrey KT20 5PD

BP House Horticultural Society
Victoria Street
London SW1E 5MJ

Bushey and District Horticultural Society
P.H. Wyatt Esq
85 Hill Way
Bushey
Watford
Herts WD2 2AF

Chingford Horticultural Society
G. Baker Esq
5 Heathcote Grove
Chingford
Essex

Chiswick Horticultural Society
G.G. Chipperfield Esq
16 Riverview Grove
Chiswick
London W4

Coutts Horticultural Society
N.J. Parsons
440 Strand
London WC2

List of Addresses

Cuffley Horticultural Society
C.C. Johns Esq
27 Burleigh Way
Cuffley
Potters Bar
Herts EN6 4LG

East Grinstead Horticultural Society
M.E. Gobey Esq
13 Stoneleigh Close
East Grinstead
Sussex RH19 3DY

Finchley Horticultural Society
12 Gordon Road
Finchley
London N3

The Forty Hill Mutual Improvement Horticultural Society
367 Baker Street
Enfield
Middlesex

Gerrards Cross Horticultural Society
D.C.C. Balfour Esq
Craigy
Fulmer Road
Gerrards Cross
Bucks

GLC Staff Horticultural Society
H.J. Luff Esq
Room 392 B
County Hall
London SE1

Hatch End Horticultural Society
E.J. Barnes Esq
27 Milne Field
Hatch End
Pinner
Middx HA5 4DP

Headley Horticultural Society
Miss C.L. Barnes, MBE
36 Phillips Crescent
Bordon
Hants

Hillingdon Show Society
D.G. Knight Esq (Treasurer)
121 Sweetcroft Lane
Hillingdon
Middx

Hitchin Horticultural Society
Norman Crick Esq
19 Cross Street
Letchworth
Herts

Hornchurch Horticultural Society
W.C. Gray Esq
26 Newlyn Avenue
Hornchurch
Essex

Hutton Horticultural Society
34 Chelmsford Road
Shenfield
Brentwood
Essex

Kenton (Middx) Horticultural Society
47 Christchurch Avenue
Kenton
Harrow
Middx

Kingswood, W. and T. Horticultural Society
Alan Jones Esq
50 Kingswood Road
Tadworth
Surrey

Marlow and District Horticultural Society
Pennymead
Bell Court
Hurley
Berks SL6 5NA

Merrow Horticultural Society
126 Bushy Hill Drive
Merrow
Guildford
Surrey

Metal Box Company Horticultural Society
The Gate
Brinkworth Road
Brinkworth
Chippenham
Wilts

Naphill Horticultural Society
P.J. Hyre Esq
'Oatley'
Main Road
Naphill
High Wycombe
Bucks

National Westminster Bank Horticultural Society
R.W. Hedge Esq
PO Box 88
2 Purley Way
Croydon
Surrey CR9 3BL

New Scotland Yard (CS) Horticultural Society
E.R. Bright Esq
Room 635
New Scotland Yard
Broadway
London SW1

Northern Horticultural Society
D. Fergusson Esq
Harlow Car Gardens
Harrogate
Yorks

Delphinium Group, Northern Horticultural Society
R. Lister Esq
North Lodge
The Heath
Long Causeway
Leeds
Yorks

List of Addresses

Norwich and Norfolk Horticultural Society
G.P. Murrell Esq
North Bay
Bungay Road
East Poringland
Norwick
Norfolk

Pinner Horticultural Society
53 Capel Gardens
Pinner
Middx

Rolvenden Gardening Society
G. Bullimore Esq (Hon. Sec.)
61 High Street
Rolvenden
Cranbrook
Kent

Roundhay (Leeds) Horticultural Society
30 Sunnyview Avenue
Leeds
Yorks LS11 8QY

RWR & Horticultural Society
R. Edwards Esq
The Cottage
Clewer Hill Lodge
Park Corner
Windsor
Berks

Sanderstead Horticultural Society
C. Kemp Esq (Hon. Sec.)
7 Arkwright Road
Sanderstead
Surrey CR2 9NL

Saxlingham and District Horticultural Society
Dr S. Griffiths (Hon. Sec.)
Hill House
Hempnall
Norwich NR15 2LP

Sevenoaks and District FA Club
19 St George's Road
Sevenoaks
Kent

Sevenoaks Horticultural Society
Lady Alison Davis
Westcot
8 Beaconside
Sevenoaks
Kent

Southgate and District Horticultural Society
Mrs H. Goodall
63 Park Avenue
Palmers Green
London N13

Borough of Southport Flower Show Department
Victoria Buildings
Lord Street
Southport
Lancs

List of Addresses

Standard Chartered Bank Horticultural Society
G. Teare Esq
10 Clements Lane
London EC4H YAB

Stone Cum Ebony Flower Show
Mrs Withers Green
Stone Corner Farm
Stone-in-Oxney
Tenterden
Kent

Surbiton Horticultural Society
R.D. Gubler Esq
93 Beresford Avenue
Tolworth
Surbiton
Surrey

Surrey Horticultural Federation
Laurian
Hill Close
Wonersh Park
Guildford
Surrey GU5 0PQ

Sutton and District Horticultural Society
5 Kayemoor Road
Sutton
Surrey SH5 3HK

Thames Valley Horticultural Society
Mrs V.L. Byles
Walnut Tree Cottage
Laleham Reach
Chertsey
Surrey KT6 8RR

Thornton Heath and Norbury Horticultural Society
The Secretary
67 Harcourt Road
Thornton Heath
Surrey

Wallington, Carshalton and Beddington Horticultural Society
105 Bute Road
Wallington
Surrey SN6 8AE

West Central Horticultural and Trading Society
Room 633
21-31 New Oxford Street
London WC1A 1AA

West Wickham Horticultural Society
A.H. Baker Esq
409 Upper Elmers End Road
Beckenham
Kent

Weybridge Horticultural Club
'Redcourt'
14 Heath Road
Weybridge
Surrey

List of Addresses

Worcester Park Horticultural Society
E.R. May Esq (Hon. Sec.)
80 Caldbeck Avenue
Worcester Park
Surrey KT4 7SH

Overseas
Canterbury Horticultural Society (Inc.)
J.C. Fraser Esq (Sec.)
213 Manchester Street
Christchurch
New Zealand

Hutt Valley Horticultural Society
PO Box 30019
Lower Hutt
New Zealand

Salisbury and District Garden Club
Mrs R. Kennedy
PO Box 1544
Salisbury
Rhodesia

Thornhill Horticultural Society
Mrs M.D. Bissell
29 Knotty Pine Trail
Thornhill
Ontario L3T 3W5
Canada

Transvaal Horticultural Society
PO Box 7616
Johannesburg
South Africa

Victoria Horticultural Society
PO Box 5081
Postal Station B
Victoria, BC
Canada

Western Res. Delphinium Society
Harvey J. Andre Esq
11328 Lake Avenue
Cleveland
Ohio 44102
USA

Index

Hybridization, 15–16, 30, 97–102

International Horticultural Congress, 115

'Janet Lucas', 23
John Innes composts, 32–3, 91
Joint Committee of The Royal Horticultural
    Society, 77
Judging, 82–4

Kelway, 17
'King of the Delphinums', 17

Lascelles, the Rev. E., 18
Langdon, Dr Brian, 25
Langdon, C.F., 18
Larkspur 11–13
Laterals, 83
Latty, Roy, 21
Legro, Dr Bob, 25
Lemoine, 16–17
Leonian, Dr, 22
Lucas, H.R. (Reg), 20

Mildew, 62
Mini–trial, 95
Moerheim Nurseries, 13

Netherlands, 24
Nitrogen, 43, 81

'Pacific' strain, 22–4, 28, 29
Parrett, Ronald, 19
Patios, 90–1

191